CONVERSATIONS

Inspirational stories full of humor,
encouragement and life-lessons.

Steve Warren

I dedicate this book to someone who created happiness for me when I was growing up, my sister Dee. As the oldest sibling, she took the time to listen and validate my opinions no matter how insignificant.

CONVERSATIONS FROM THE PORCH

In today's world, we often miss out on personal conversations. There sure is a lot of texting going on. My old fingers are no longer nimble when I try to text, and sometimes words don't come out spelled correctly. Many times, I've had to delete and start over because using an incorrect word in place of a similar sounding word could get one into trouble. Not to mention the times I am trying to a make a point and it takes on a whole new meaning when I type the wrong letter. So here goes…take a seat as I share with you my conversation of the day.

Right now, my mind is wrestling between my wants and my needs. I don't know about you, but I still have dreams and goals to achieve. Sometimes it feels like they are sailing on a slow ship from China. In the Bible it reads, "Knock and the door will be opened to you." Knock-knock, my knuckles are raw. But I cannot give up. Have any of you ever been there too? Yeah, I have more times than I want to admit. Still, something deep inside of me refuses to give up, will not let go. I can't, and I hope you can't and won't either. We must forge ahead if we want our dreams to come true. I often talk to God and ask Him about His plans for me. Maybe if our lives were picture perfect there would be no reason to depend on GOD.

My late uncle, who fought during World War II, used to say that there weren't any atheists in fox holes. Calling out to God was a frequent occurrence. You know, it might sound crazy, but I don't think a perfect life would work here after all; it's a temporary place - a voyage, an adventure - and you might end up checking out kicking and screaming because you do not want to leave. I believe that one day my journey will lead to a perfect forever place. But right now, I am still on this planet called Earth searching for answers to my prayers. Some have already materialized, and some have not. Timing is everything. There may come a day when I will thank God for unanswered prayers. Nevertheless, my binoculars are out. Has anyone seen my ship? SHINE everyone!!!

FAITH

People often speak about famous personalities who have inspired their lives. These iconic people are usually in the sports or entertainment industries. The media is constantly buzzing around them, interviewing and taking their photographs. Publicity is a must for people who want to be in the limelight. For me, the most inspirational person would be, hands–down, the late Rose Kennedy: a woman who lost four children in horrific situations yet kept her poise, dignity and strength during the trials and storms of her life. When an interviewer asked her what the most important thing in her life was, the answer did not include looks, money, or social position. She said it was her FAITH! I must say, I wholeheartedly agree. Honestly, I admit questioning many things in my life. In my early education at a private school, I'm sure when my name appeared on the teachers roll the nuns holding that piece of paper probably wanted to flee the country! Why? Because I was forever asking "why?" And it will not be a big surprise to you who know me that at the ripe age of 63, I am still asking why? Why is this world so UN-fair, why is there death and destruction all around us and why is there so much pain and suffering? After all this time I still don't have the answers, and I'm not even close.

What I can tell you is that I believe GOD loves us, all of us. GOD has been my life preserver and FAITH has been my anchor. It is not always easy to live in this crazy revolving world. When I insist to people that God is real, they usually counter with "prove it." I try to tell them, "Just look around and tell me what you see." Can anyone deny the astounding creations on earth and in the Universe? Majestic mountains, endless valleys, global oceans, cornucopia of animals, stars, galaxies, and least we forget...humans, created in God's image. True, we often hear about all the horrendous things too, like wars, natural disasters, and people going hungry. Here we go again, "why?" Fortunately, in my life many wonderful people have been sent to guide me, teach me and show me love. And if I listen quietly...sometimes GOD speaks to me.

I remember when I was teaching my oldest son how to swim, he would reach out and grab me saying, "Daddy, I'm scared, I'm scared." Now even as a grown man, I reach out to my father - my Heavenly Father - and say, "Help me I'm scared." Friends, I don't know what I would do without my faith; it is priceless! I am a flesh man and a spirit man. The flesh man must learn to surrender, and as we talk, this process of life is ongoing. But the spirit man...the spirit man is ever so young and still growing. I talk with GOD often like I did when I was a small boy, and of course the "why?" question comes forth. Fortunately, my Heavenly Father is patient, kind and loving. My faith is grounded in the fact that God loves me despite all my flaws. He loves me and above all else wishes me a good life. God desires this for you also. Everything in this life will fade away, so hold on tight to your FAITH. It will sustain you through the tough times. Let it be your rock and foundation even in the darkest nights. Like Rose Kennedy, it is the most important thing to me. Have a great day, my friends. Keep the faith and let your light SHINE!!!

HERE COMES THE SUN

Does anyone here remember the childhood fable about poor Henny Penny? She was the chicken little who screamed, "The sky is falling, the sky is falling!" I certainly do, and I believe most of the people in my generation do as well. In this sometimes-chaotic world, one needs to take his or her nerve medication before reading or listening to any news. It's frightening! The world around us is a scary place, full of doom and gloom predictions. And to add to the confusion, too many fingers are pointing out who our enemies are and who our friends are, expecting us to accept what they believe. Even the politicians are painting fearful pictures of their rivals ("Vote for that one and you're going to regret it forever."). If I were to take everything as fact, I'd build a fall-out shelter and close the door behind me on the world. BUT I'd miss out on the whole point of being here to do what I'm supposed to do and do well. That, my friend, also holds true for you. We are not put here to be like Grandmother's fine china, spending our days in the china cupboard to be admired and not used for fear we might be broken. Yes, it's a tough place to dwell in, planet Earth. Anything can happen and it might, but I myself consider life to be a precious, rare gift. I don't want to miss a moment in living out my purpose...to spread hope, reach out to other people, and to love them with a full heart. Surprise, it is your purpose too. We are all in this world to help each other step by step. It doesn't have to be earth-shaking; even small gestures such as being kind, being thoughtful, and being understanding can make big difference. You may think something small is inconsequential, but it can create a domino effect of positive thoughts moving into the mechanisms of everyday life. I cannot think of a better way to convey your purpose. Will the sky really fall? It might someday, but here is the GOOD news about it. While the sun was shining, while the birds were singing, while my life was moving, I LIVED in the best way possible. Friends, please don't live in fear of the bad things that might happen. Instead, live as though anything GOOD might happen. Work hard so it can and believe it will...for you and everyone around you. Your life is important; you have so much to contribute. Go forth into the sunlight and SHINE!!!

FINDING HAPPINESS
IN AN UNHAPPY WORLD

We all have different ideas on many subjects, but I do believe we would all agree on one subject: "It is important to be happy." Someone once told me that happiness should not require work, that it should just "be there." I don't know, but I DO think we have to put some effort into the mix, especially when we find ourselves in everyday uphill battles. What do we battle over? Our personal problems, our friends and loved one's circumstances and, in general, the very world around us. When things become cloudy, we can't see where the road to happiness lies. I wish I had the recipe it takes to be happy so I could give out free samples. I would like that very much. But I can't, and unfortunately neither can anyone else. The problem is most of the time we are frantically searching outside of ourselves when ironically the answer lies within.

One of my favorite lines comes from the movie "The Wizard of Oz." At the end of the movie, Dorothy was told that she could have gone home any time she wished...it was inside her the whole time. In my opinion, happiness IS within you, and it has been there all the time. Definitely an inside job...you just have to seek it. True, it's wonderful - more than wonderful - when someone in your life can make you feel happy. But I think you need to find that place first, and the beautiful gift of sharing it follows. I try to keep happiness simple.

A while ago I planted a sunflower seed in my garden. The poor little thing was struggling to bloom - like we do at times - but yesterday, out popped the flower, bright and beautiful. This made me very happy. Friends, I hope you will find happiness in this day within your heart. It belongs to you, without judgment, fear or any explanation necessary. I believe it has always been inside you. So be brave, be bold, own it and use it wisely...SHINE!!!

THE POWER OF LOVE

The years I experienced as a letter carrier were some of the most rewarding and interesting times in my life. It was then that I became very "interested" in people and knew that I was destined to be a "people person." Perhaps because I cared and listened, people would share their stories with me (which would make an interesting book in itself). On one of my routes I met a woman who had a "Type A" personality...nice, but to the point, and not drawn into drama. But the story she told me was thought-provoking. Today, I'm going to apply this story to MOTHER'S DAY and dedicate it to the eternal, driving force of care and love that is second nature to being a mother. This woman lived in a mobile home. She told me that one morning after she got ready to go to work, she was drinking her cup of coffee and happened to look out of her front window. She could not believe her eyes when she saw her mother, who had passed away some years ago, walking around the yard and motioning to her. The woman quickly put her coffee cup down and ran outside, eager to see her mother. But when she got out there, the vision had disappeared. Disappointed, she turned around and saw thick smoke coming out of the rear of her home. Her house was on fire! If she had not ran outside that day, she might not have seen the smoke. She was positive that her mother had appeared in order to save her life. Was it really her mother or just an apparition? I don't know. Is it possible for the dead to communicate with us? Perhaps, but what I do know is that the love dwelling in a mother's heart is a very omnipotent force.

My own mother was a prayer warrior and I can HONESTLY tell you I feel the presence of her prayers for me now, even though she passed away many years ago. LOVE is eternal, and no one can measure the power that comes with it. The power of a mother who loves their child is boundless. HAPPY MOTHER'S DAY! And do not forget to SHINE!!!

THE PERFECT AGE

A few days ago, I was talking with a friend of mine who is my age. We were discussing what we thought would be the perfect age to live to. My friend has great ambitions and I hope to see them all come to fruition. I have come into contact with some really impressive older people in my journey of late. Take, for instance, one sweet lady who eventually passed away at 100 years young. She was alert, vibrant and still driving a car until a couple of years back. But I have also met some people in their late sixties who have a tough time dealing with life on a day to day basis. I am going to be honest with you: today I look at aging in a different light and a different weight. I believe I'm here with assignments, projects and tasks to accomplish from the moment of my birth to the day I will die. Life's activities should be performed with enjoyment and, of course, with love mixed in there too; but maybe it's not the quantity of the time, rather the quality. Life is a mystery. Life is a gift - a most precious one - and few really want to leave this familiar place. Some wonder where the path leads to, most believe it leads to a higher place. Different people have different ideas, but I'll say this: "Life is like having a full plate...finish what there is, and then you may have more." Life really never stops, it goes on. To what, to where and how I really can't say, so for me, my friend, I'm not worried about how long I have, rather that I finish what's on my plate. I've been a lucky boy. The menu has been full and rich, no complaints here. Right now, I am sure of this moment and looking forward to a "helping" of the day. Whenever and whatever evening brings, I say bring it on!! Value your time, porcupine, and...SHINE!!!

NEXT IN LINE

My favorite saying is, "We are things of the day!" I interpret this as...our lives move quickly, like a day does, so do what you want to do now - what you *must* do now - and don't take a second for granted. Men, I believe, more than women, are vain creatures who revel in their strength. It will be a very sad day when we will have to accept help from someone else with activities of daily living. But friends, we are creatures of the flesh who are subject to the click of the clock named Time. Somewhere out there, I believe there is a small child preparing to take my place in line, and I am alright with that; it's good and the way it should be. So, while I'm still at the front of the line, I'm gonna shine before Father Time yells out "NEXT!" Come on, get up, get dressed and get in line. Life is calling! Keep moving and remember to be kind 'cause there will always be someone else NEXT in line, so SHINE!!!

YOU MIGHT FALL ON YOUR FACE

A very famous socialite once said she believed in "fate" but added, "You have to show up for it." I like that, I do. To some degree I agree with her, but I'd rather say this: I believe in opportunities and yes, you do have to show up. It can be a scary world out there; critics are everywhere waiting to pounce.

Years ago, I was in the production of "Fiddler on the Roof" and, as usual, in a supporting role. In this play I had to perform the bottle dance and as the opening grew closer, my fears escalated. I will never forget the lesson I learned. I was telling the costume lady that I was afraid I would make a mistake and screw things up. Her reply struck a chord. I believe her exact words were "I don't care if you get out there and fall flat on your face!" In other words, a lot of people - including me - had put their blood, sweat, and tears into the production, but the show must go on! She went on to scold, "I've spent weeks working on your costume and you're gonna do it!" Plain and simple, no sympathy. Those words would carry me through life. Yes, I may fall on my face when I put myself "out there." Nevertheless, I must get out there and do it!

Many of us look back at situations in our lives wishing we had taken the chance and accepted challenging opportunities. Much like acting, putting ourselves out there with the spotlight on our face is not easy. We might be a hit or might be a flop. Now I try not to say no to any possibilities, but - fate be darned - here goes. True confession: I have fallen flat on my face at one time or another. But I got up and continued on, as you must do. Be brave soldiers. Life is calling, so put on your costume and give the performance of your life. You never know who might be sitting out in the audience. Bravo, SHINE!!!

MIND, HEART AND SOUL

Belief, faith and love do not live under a roof within walls or in material possessions, rather they live within the mind, the heart and the soul where no force of nature can destroy them. Dear friends, we are living in a most extraordinary time where the forces of good and evil are at war. It is possible to rise above in goodness, light and with great LOVE in our hearts. Victory is within our faith in the one true GOD. I BELIEVE...it's the time to SHINE!!!

GETTING THE JOB DONE

Have you ever been in a restaurant with friends and it's so noisy that you can't hear what's being said? I think our lives can be much like that. There are so many distractions around us that we don't listen to our inner voice. Yes, it's there; the secret is to listen. Do not overlook the obvious; let your inner voice be your ship's rudder. Maybe we simply don't know *how* to listen to it. I'm working on it ever so carefully. Funny, it's been there all the time and yet I've never appreciated it. Trust in yourself and listen to what steers the boat. WHO you are is the most valuable gift you can offer to the world. Everything is really deep inside you, every tool you need to get the job done. Work on you, 'cause YOU SHINE!!!

ANGELS IN THE OUTFIELD

I have told some of you this story more than once, but it's a great one and worth repeating (even more so because it goes along with my belief that there are people put in our lives for learning purposes, if we pay attention). When I think about it, there have been many people who have been put in my life who molded my thought processes since day one, and not by accident.

Take, for instance, my first real paying job. I was going to turn sixteen that year, so I announced to my parents that I'd like a car of my own. Crickets...no offers came forth. My personal financial adviser was an old piggy bank as empty as a cookie jar in the summertime. My mother took me (almost by hand) to a local restaurant where I was offered the glorified position of being a dishwasher. Jackpot - my car was right around the corner. But before my car arrived, one very important lesson made its appearance. The heat from the hot night was streaming through the screen door at the back of the kitchen. A man knocked on the door, and I walked back there. Dressed in very dirty clothes, he looked like he had not shaved or had a bath in days. He announced that he was hungry and inquired if we had any leftovers. I went to the owner, a mature gentleman who was in the front talking with paying customers. I waited until my boss was finished before telling him about the man at the door. The owner said nothing to me but went back there right away. The tattered man was still there, and I watched as he repeated the request. Then something wonderful happened. The owner told the man to follow him. My jaw dropped as my boss seated the hungry man at one of the best tables in the establishment and told him to order anything he wanted...anything. Later that night, my boss opened the door and told me I could go home. Before leaving, I asked him, "Why, sir, did you do that? Why did you bring that bum into your restaurant, put him at one of the best tables and give him a free dinner?" He told me quite frankly, "Young man, you never know when an angel might come to your door and test you."

I don't know if I got it "then" but fast forward many years later. Recently when I was working at my part-time job, someone tapped me on the shoulder. I turned around and saw a young, messy man in dirty clothes holding what looked like a Dollar Store hot dog. He asked me, rather frankly, if I would please microwave it for him. He looked like he might have been on a labor-pool type of job. I gazed ever so closely into his eyes. I had seen eyes like that before, like a ghost from the past.

Point being, I believe we all get a chance to do good, to be an "Earth Angel" to someone along the way. Take the time to show your love and to care for someone less fortunate than you. Don't miss your opportunity, my friends; seize the moment, pass the test! There are angels in the outfield. By the way, I finally did get my car, a Volkswagen beetle. Wish I still had it today and could be sixteen all over again...scratch that, just give me the car. SHINE ON TO A GREAT DAY!!!

LIGHTS, CAMERA, ACTION

LIFE is very much like a play. In the first act, you aren't always sure of what is going on. By act two you should realize where it's going, and after the curtain falls you should get the gist of the story. But you really do need to pay attention.

Once, when I was playing a part in another theatrical performance and reciting my bit piece of dialog, I looked down into the first row and saw an elderly man sleeping. Apparently, my performance did the job better than any sleeping pill. Most of the time in real life I was comfortable in accepting mediocre roles. And now, here I am in the midst of this production and gosh-darn the mediocre! I decided to go full steam ahead with the realization that while I may never be the leading man, the stage was mine at that moment and I was going to give my best performance and "SHINE." I know my place, and it's alright to be a "character." In fact, I am having a good time with it. If you meet me in person you might say, "What a character!"

Friends, pay attention to your life and be good to yourself. Know your part, accept it and play it for all you've got. I guarantee that no one is going to fall asleep when I'm on the stage anymore! It is all about having a good time. Hope you will too. Till the final curtain goes down, live your life to the fullest and you will SHINE!!!

GOD HANGS OUT IN THE HOOD

Take note of this very important lesson: Angels do have dirty faces sometimes, and this one had a mouth full of "colorful" words to go with it. When you serve the public, as I have for a very long time, it can be the greatest education, hands down. I've seen almost everything. The good, the bad and the ugly are all out there. It's also the best education that I have ever received. Some people out there would shock a church service if they showed up wearing inappropriate outfits and spewing out colorful words.

When I was young, I went to a very strict religious-based elementary school, a denomination I was raised in since I was born. Today I realize how fortunate I was to have received a Christian education, although I will also tell you that I look at things in a whole different light now that I am older.

In school, I was always the one asking questions: why this or why that? My first-grade teacher (a nun) left the school after Christmas. I'm sure I had nothing to do with it. There was a rumor that before each school year the nuns drew straws to see who would get me in their class. I had a teacher once whose name was Sister Mary Augustine and I liked to call her Sister Madagascar. You need not wonder why they were always asking me to draw a picture a picture of hell. Look at it this way: after having me in their class, everything must have been heavenly after I moved on. And my idea about God was that He was this "man" who was, at any time, waiting behind a cloud to strike me down when I did anything wrong. The teachers talked about hell sometimes and it scared the hell out of me, still does. I felt like I would never be good enough. I thought that if I didn't go to church there would be an "X" beside my name somewhere, some place. I think all my teachers were wonderful people who strove to impart their beliefs to me, but somewhere along the line I took a different path to analyze my way of thinking. For instance, I don't know what GOD looks like or how He thinks, but I have found Him in UN-likely places and in some people who might look questionable to the "religious" world.

For example, there was a woman who I will call Annie. Annie was a tough customer, a big woman with wild hair and a crazy laugh. Her home looked like Fred Sanford's junk shop. It had a couple of abandoned cars in the yard and several dogs (she called each one Baby) running about. This was one of my first mail routes, one that no one else really wanted. The neighborhood was literally in the "hood." Looking back, it was just what the doctor ordered. I would learn that "God" hangs out - big time - in the hood. Annie would have been tossed out of most churches for using four letter words but hear this...I saw "GOD" in her. She was the most honest person I have ever met. And although she had, as she said, "did time" she honestly said, "I deserved it!" As tough as she was, after I told her about my children one day she would often bring out a bag of cookies from the Dollar Store (she was as poor as a church mouse) and tell me, "Give 'em to your kids and tell 'em I love them."

Friends, I am not trying to knock any form of organized religion but just want to say that I saw GOD in places where many would not choose to go. We all have to be careful about who we think are the "chosen ones." GOD is so awesome; He sees what we can't. Now go out there and SHINE!!!

PROTEIN FOR THE SOUL

We need to be careful about what we allow in our thought processes: what we see, what we read and all the places we let our mind go to, just like right here, online. Protect your mind. The brain works overtime; it never ever stops, and it filters out in dreams. This high-tech computer keeps everything going. I worry for the young people today, digesting all those violent games they play online. Then there are television shows on true crime and even [gulp] the REAL news we hear every day. IT DOES AFFECT OUR THOUGHT PROCESSES. If I were to raise children again, I'd ban violent games, and I might not even have a television set. A young mind should be protected. YOU ARE WHAT YOU THINK.

So here I am kids, with my mission to try to impart positive thoughts into your life, and here you are. You need to, and you must, snuff out the negative, because positive thoughts are...protein for the soul. We can't hide from the world; we just have to be careful about what we allow in. Take the trash outside where it belongs, not in our living rooms, not in our minds. Here is my advice: start the day in prayer of thanksgiving for all the good things in your life. Don't be afraid to ask for help and guidance; everybody needs help at some time or other. Listen to your favorite music and put some exercise into the mix by dancing. Set in your mind a simple goal for your day. It will give you a sense of accomplishment. Surround yourself with positive people who bounce off positive energy. OWN YOUR THOUGHT PROCESSES. As you think, so you are! My thoughts for you...have a great day, enjoy YOU and do good for others. I try to live by my words. Now I am off to the gym and thinking, *Wow, thank you, GOD, for another day.* SHINE!!!

SECRETS IN THE SOUL

There is so much freedom in knowing who you really are without seeking approval from anyone. Who YOU are has nothing to do with what you look like or where you came from. We are encased in individual bodies in this life form. Those who cannot see the interior, or choose not to make the effort, usually don't venture beyond what the eyes show them. So many miss the true message and it is so sad. It is the SOUL that lies within each of us that truly carries the purpose.

My earthly eyes are fading, yet my spiritual eyes are seeing things that I never noticed before. Layers of truth are shedding before me. WE are subject to the physical forms but so few of us go beyond. If we did, we would see a light revolving in the deep recesses of our soul. Everything we touch and everything we see in this dimension is really only a mirage. Like the set of a play or movie, it will all be torn down one day when the purpose is over. What lies in the soul, the heart of the person, will be eternal.

Dear friends, when you look at each other, try to go beyond what you see and look with LOVE upon the soul in other people. Someone recently accused me of being gullible, an easy target, perhaps naive. It's alright, no problem, I understand. I don't seek approval, do not need it. I am ME being ME and honestly having a good time at it. I hope the same for each and every one of you. So, look beyond because that is where we are all heading and do not forget to SHINE!!!

DISCIPLINE AND RESPECT

It was a very disturbing story and someone in the classroom filmed it. A strong young man, a student, was fighting with his male teacher and the teacher was struggling to stand his ground. It was a most sad moment in time because this student was physically showing disrespect for an elder and a teacher.

A thought brings me back in time. Summer was over and it was fifth grade, 1966. Everyone was excited to meet our new teacher. In comes this nun (I will not give you her name, partly out of fear because if she hears me from the heavens talking about her, she might paddle my behind to the moon and back). She was a tough, very small woman in statue who possessed supernatural abilities like no one I'd ever met. She had eyes in back of her head, and I really believed she could read your mind too. The marines had nothing on her. She could parachute faster than a lightning bolt from her chair to my desk and pull me by my ear to get my attention when I was daydreaming. But I can't deny that she was a good teacher. She wanted all of us to succeed in life. It was Boot Camp 101. If one of us did not do our homework, she would send home a report making sure our parents were aware of the situation and then [gulp] they had to sign the form. One fine day, there was a small group of us who received our unacceptable reports. One of us, it might have been me (I had some ideas in those days, and this was a beaut) would sign each other's slip with a so-called "authentic" signature of our parents. It should have been a cake walk, and the way I looked at it no one would get hurt. The next morning our little group was called to her desk, a most feared location. Attila the Hun asked each one of us, "Did your parents sign this?" The look on our faces was priceless. But, so was the look on her face, one that read, "Oh really, do you expect ME to buy this?" Then each of us stuck out our hand waiting for the paddle. Now days, the teacher would get arrested. Back then you prayed your parents didn't get wind of it because if they did, you'd get another whack at home. Do I think she was right? Head on! It was valuable a lesson in discipline and respect. We knew what was expected of us: to honor our elders and teachers.

As a nation, we have sadly strayed from respecting authority. I know that we have all heard all types of horror stories as well. I'm sure some are true, but this dear woman dedicated her life to teaching. I see a lack of respect for so much authority today. You need not approve of the person, but RESPECT the position, from the president on down the line. I mean this: a society cannot survive without respect. It's been a lifetime since I was that skinny little boy sitting at a school desk, but when I think of that fierce little woman with love, I say, "thank you" for all the tough, valuable lessons you taught me...and yes, I am trying to pay attention. I still like to daydream...some days are better than others. Oh well, have a good day, friends. SHINE ON!!!

THOUGHTS ARE VERY POWERFUL

When I worked as a letter carrier, there was a stamp that we would put on certain unclaimed letters that read "Return to Sender-Unknown at this Address." It is a sure-proof way to deal with negative thoughts: not at this address, not in this soul, no way. I would say, for most of us, our thought processes are much like the mail: some are FIRST class thoughts, others 3rd class, and bulk or "JUNK MAIL" thoughts thrown in there for good measure. Some very fortunate people are good at sorting them out and, sadly, some are not.

During my early years, I allowed many negative thoughts about myself to be delivered First Class. I accepted them because my self-esteem was in the junk mail pile. It can happen to anyone. But slowly over time, by the grace of GOD and living long enough,

I came to realize the truth. I began to see the "light" and this is a true story. One fine day I was thinking negative thoughts and a VOICE - a very, very distinctive voice - came from deep inside my mind and said, "ONLY IF YOU ALLOW IT." Yes, the negative will come and try to stay and even plant bad seeds, but ONLY if YOU will allow it. Friends, WE CANNOT ALLOW IT! There is NO room at the inn for negative thoughts IN YOUR THINKING PROCESSES. YOU have the power to block it, so BLOCK THEM. Develop a method in the way you think and then in what YOU say. Thoughts are powerful and the words that you use are the cement to make them work. You were wonderfully created for success. GOD, your Creator, wants you to succeed, flourish and to accomplish what you were sent here to do. And I, who have never met many of you, wish it for you too...a happy and successful life. It ALL begins with your thought process - when you think, feel, and live positive, thinking POSITIVE thoughts become what you think you are. With only good thoughts upon each and every one of you, have a good day and SHINE ON TO VICTORY!!!

SWEET DREAMS

One night, I had a very interesting dream. I saw my late father, only he was much, much younger as in pictures I have seen of him. He had nice straight black hair and he looked amazingly young and healthy. In the dream, I walked up to him and told him how great he looked, much younger than I do now. It felt strange to be calling this young man "Dad." I don't know if the dead can communicate with us or if it was all in my head, but I must tell you, it was beyond nice.

As I become older, there is a full cast of loved ones and friends who have gone beyond the stars. I think of them all often and I miss them, but I realize it's all part of living and dying. We bloom, we shine and then we go. My greatest message, and my greatest belief, is to SHINE in the TIME we have! To be honest with you, as awesome as I believe the "other side" will be, I've got work to do here. I don't want to leave any rock UN-turned, get 'er done! And when the time comes, I can pack my bags and leave, knowing that I have done the best I could with all that I was given.

My father was my best friend, hands down. I hope he is young, strong and happy in his new life. I really believe life never really stops; it only gets better. But, then, that is my dream, isn't it? For now, I'm here, and there is no time to "sleep" through it. I'm up and getting ready to "rock" my day. SHINE everyone!!!

ENID THE SNAKE

Yesterday afternoon in my garden I saw my old friend, a long, black snake I call Enid (and I'm sure Enid has a name for me too!). Anyway, Enid has been a resident here for quite a few years now. We have an arrangement: when Enid comes out, I stay in and when I come out, Enid stays...wherever Enid stays. Sometimes we do meet up and it's an awkward moment when usually one of us slithers away. Enid is one of many critters in my yard. There is the squirrel who hangs upside down while robbing the bird feeder, and there is a bird singing in my tree - or is it the bird's tree? Point here, we ALL share this space. Before my house was here the property was an orange grove, and before that probably woods, and all those creatures - great and small - lived here. Enid's great-great-great grandfather probably held court here. We all share this planet. You know, the snake might think he owns the place, though I pay the taxes! The bird and the squirrel might have something to say about that, too. I mean, we all have a vested interest in this place. I, too, think it's all mine.

The TRUTH is, we are all just visitors and need to be respectful of each other. I try to be. Enid seems to have a stubborn streak. The other day I was clipping the hedges and out came the head, almost to say, "Hey, I'm trying to sleep here, tone it down!!!" In a crazy way, we all need each other, and we all have a purpose under GOD'S sun, all creatures great and small. SHINE EVERYONE!!!

ORGANIC SUMMERS

The other day, a person was in agony over the summer's heat and boy I do understand. By noon, my work shirt was wet from being outside in the bright sun and scorching heat. But then I began to remember the summer days of yesterday, gone.

I grew up in an age where most homes did not have air conditioning even though it was in the sunny and often humid state of south Florida. I grew up on the "wrong side of the tracks" so to speak. We lived in an old wooden house that had a giant ceiling fan. If I close my eyes, I can still hear the "whoosh" sound when it would go on, and since there was little or no crime, you kept the windows open at night hoping for a breeze to come along. They were simple summer days. Each year we would get two pairs of shoes: a sensible pair to wear to school and a dress pair for church. And then in the summer, I would get a pair of black and white sneakers, and they had to last all summer. So many times, I'd run barefoot down the dirt road and then shuffle through the grass. Today, many people look for organic food and vegetables. I understand, but back then it wasn't an issue, at least not for me. I drank out of a garden hose from a well, I picked cherries from a neighbor's hedge and I even ate cheap hot dogs raw. Guess what people? I'm still here. We did not play electronic games; there was no such thing around. My mother wanted us kids out of the house. We'd ride our bikes and we build tree forts and make "organic" fun out of nothing. Our father used to bring home old, empty oil barrels from work, and we would pretend that we were rolling logs, and he made us homemade wooden stilts to walk around on for simple fun. One summer, my sister decided that we needed a pool. The neighbors had two older daughters who had a small, vinyl free-standing pool that they didn't use anymore. My sister decided that we should buy it. "With what?" I asked. We searched every piggy bank in the entire house up and down. I can't tell you how much it came to, but it wasn't much, so my sister became a savvy negotiator that would marvel the likes of Wall Street. I would watch her go back and forth until finally she closed the deal of the century. To be honest, the neighbors probably felt sorry for us. But in our minds, we were the high rollers in this deal. We hit pay dirt. I think she came to me and said, "Let's go get it!" We struggled to bring our gold mine home. Two skinny kids dragging the pool home across a field determined to get it home was priceless. Now, "Let the good times begin!" Our father must have helped us put it together, and when the garden hose came on, we ran to get into our primitive swim gear. It was heaven on earth, especially on those hot sweltering summer days. They were sweet, innocent days, and when I think of them, I smile. In the world we live in today we are told that organic foods are healthier for you and good children's shoes cost more than my father made all summer long. Oh, how the times have changed. I remember the innocent days of youth and I smile. I wouldn't have missed those days for the entire world. Sometimes at night, when I hear the crickets singing, my thoughts go back there, and I think I hear the sound of our fan sucking up the hot air in that old wooden house. But then my AC unit kicks on and I feel the crisp cold air. Now "that's cool" sure beats the heck out of that old ceiling fan! It's nice to remember the past, but the present sure can be a present! SHINE everyone!!!

NEW HORIZONS

In the last few years, young families have been moving into our neighborhood and it's like a fresh, new chapter has begun. I like seeing and hearing the children play; It reminds me of my own life some decades ago. I was fortunate to witness all my children's births, and I can tell you, even at birth they come out with a distinct personality. Despite the fact that they were all raised the same, each one is unique. I am not an expert on any subject, but I can honestly tell you that there are patterns already in place when they come off the assembly line. Not to mention how environments, teachings, and the culture of the home get all mixed together as the child grows. It makes me sad to see that in some cultures, children are taught to hate. I don't know of any task more important than that of raising a child. I think if I had to do it over again there would be things I would change, but we gave it all we could. I took the job seriously and my wife was a fantastic mother!!! I also learned some very important lessons along the way. One, you think you are the one doing the teaching when just raising a child tends to teach YOU a few things. I know I taught them to love and to respect. **Children have been the most important "assignment" I'll ever have.** I miss those early days (though not always the teenage ones but it comes with the territory).

I can remember the show of late entertainer, Art Linkletter, where he interviewed young children and the funny things they would say. I remember many, many years ago when I worked as a letter carrier, and a small boy on my route was fascinated with the mail delivery. When asked what he wanted to be when he grew up, he smiled and said, "A mail truck!!!" We laughed but we knew what he meant! He is probably a C.E.O. today somewhere in the business world. Ahhh, my postal children, all grown up now…and my own too, just like it should be. Have a great day kids, and don't forget to SHINE!!!

THE GIFT OF LIFE

Time is kind of funny. As we become older, our vision is not as strong and yet we begin to see LIFE much clearer. Our hearing is not as keen, yet often, if we stay silent, we hear our inner voice talking to us. We have trouble walking, yet we know the correct pathway so, so much better. The physical form is in surrender and what has always been inside comes forth, and the famous old term comes forth: "If I only knew then what I know now." Don't know about you, but sometimes I question my past. Why did I do that or why didn't I do that? It's normal when we look in the rearview mirror of our lives. Still, backing up can get you in trouble if you don't pay attention, because seeing all the "stuff" behind us can be a scary thing, so back up carefully! Keep in mind that going forward is really the goal.

One day I was discussing how inexpensive a muscle car was when I was a young man, way, way back then. The young man I was talking to said, "Why didn't you buy that Z-28?" My answer was, "Because it took all I had to swing a Volkswagen Bug!" It's true; it would have been interesting to SEE AND HEAR the future back in our past, but then it would have been all too busy with lessons not learned. Don't beat yourself up with your past, just look at what there is today. Listen to the very beauty of nature and walk towards the future with gratitude and thanksgiving for a chance at this wonderful gift called LIFE. Everything that we've ever experienced has brought us here, so make "here" the best place yet! SHINE everyone!!!

NEED MONEY FOR A

NEW ROCKING CHAIR

You know, life really is all about the way you look at it. Some time ago a woman made me laugh at her remarks. She said it was a shame that older people [was she talking about me because I was standing right next to her?] had to work in their "older years." She added, "You know, they should have handled their money better." I could not help but howl later. Maybe I should volunteer to pose for the poster that will hang in high schools. They could use my picture with a big caption that reads "Do well in school and make good money so you don't end up like this!" Well?

Look, I suppose if you saw me in my old truck and dressed like I usually do you might mistake me for Jed Clampett (but look what he was worth!). I'm not in the

Fortune Five Hundred group but I don't have to worry about what's for dinner! I am very fortunate to work part-time at a wonderful place where I can meet wonderful people, which is one of my favorite things to do. I am a blessed man and I know it. I hope I can go on doing something while the sun is shining down on me. At one time in my young life, I thought thirty-five was "old" then fifty, and [gulp] sixty! Now I see so many active, older folks living large and looking good. Bring it on! But just in case things go south, I'll make a cardboard sign, "Too old to work, need money for a new rocking chair!" I'll leave you at that. Rocking on with my bad self. SHINE!!!

THE HAPPINESS LIST

These days, I must confess I am not as sharp as in days past. I need to make lists if my wife sends me to the store. So, I make a list and EVEN then - yes, sorry to say - I screw it up. I definitely need to edit them and make them shorter and easier to read. Then I started to think about my list for HAPPINESS. I have made it shorter too because what made me happy at one time is no longer paramount. I've been blessed to have had nice homes, cars and a good job...very blessed. But now in my mature years, I believe I have to be realistic and get right to the point in my search for that golden word HAPPINESS. I need to realize so many things on that "once upon a time list" really didn't make me slaphappy like I thought they would. It's like in the "Wizard of Oz" when the good witch told Dorothy that she had the power to go home all along, but she didn't realize it. We have the power to be happy if we only realize it. The problem is that early on we are often told what will make us happy.

My late father was a simple man who never really put a value on any material object to make him happy. He lived in an old, simple house and never really owned any valuable things. But he had a deep enduring love for his family and was a good friend to many people, and a law-abiding good citizen of this world. Before he passed away, he told me, "I've had a happy, happy life" and added if given the chance he'd live it all just the same way over again without changing a thing. His list was a short one, so I'm editing mine, as days are passing quickly: to love God, my family, my friends, and to be a good citizen of the world. Everything else I'm kind of borrowing anyway. Someday this home will belong to someone else, my vehicle will probably end up being a refrigerator and a couple of microwaves and all the material objects will be scattered like dust. But the LIST that lives in my heart, the true core of my being will say, "Be thankful for all that you have been given!" I am, and ever, ever so much more, AMEN. Have a great day my friends, SHINE!!!

BRUSH IT OFF

Luke 12-7 says, "Indeed the very hairs on your head are numbered, don't be afraid, you are worth more than the sparrows." In my case, I'm making it easy for GOD: not much hair there, so He won't have to work hard counting. My thought is this: we do live in a dangerous world; there IS death and destruction all around us. All you have to do is look at the headlines. We have alarms, warning labels, airbags and cameras everywhere to keep us safe. Now that's a good thing, but we can't dwell in a hovel that resembles a bubble. We have to go out and live. Some are so afraid of dying that they forget how to live, laugh and love each other. Might I say because this is not the way you want it to be, you hold back from enjoying WHAT IS. And that, my friend, is one hell of a note, so LIVE for what there is! I can't tell everything in my life is peaches and cream. There are, at times, some rotten eggs in the lot. That's LIFE, right? Even though I have not found a product to keep my hair from falling out I still have the floor where I can brush it off!! And, so can you; brush off the negative, the fear, the disappointment about what you have and what you don't have. BE happy and LIVE in what there is...LET YOUR LIGHT SHINE BRIGHT!!!

OLD JEANS AND A COLORFUL T-SHIRT

This story starts out dark and morbid, but stick with me, friends - it was another lesson learned. As a letter carrier, I moved around to different cities, and one of my routes brought me to deliver mail to a well-known beautiful cemetery and funeral home. I would drive through the immaculate, manicured grounds and go through the back entrance at the loading dock. There I would go to a back service door and into a long hallway past the embalming rooms.

One day as I passed, I noticed a hamper out by the hall. It had a pair of blue jeans just like I often wear, and a tee shirt similar to many of mine. My mind raced...those could have easily been my clothes; it could have been me in that room. Sounds dark, sounds morbid, sounds like the truth.

We never know friends, this thing called life, this thing called a day, an hour, a minute. It is all on loan, and in my opinion, it is meant to be used for cultivating good. I suppose we take for granted that it's just a given that tomorrow will come. But really, we don't know. Maybe today is given and nothing more. Believe it or not, coming upon this occurrence changed my thinking forever. I value every single second I live in, and I sprinkle it with thanksgiving in my heart, hope and happiness.

People often say, "You always seen so happy." You bet ya! While there is time, I plan to use it for doing good. I realize not everything is perfect in my world or in anyone else's, but friends, we all have the precious gift of life and the responsibility of using it wisely. Embrace the joys of living and sprinkle a little sugar on top. My mother always said you can catch more flies with sugar than you can with vinegar.

Right now, I'm up early and my little dog is sitting next to me patiently waiting to be fed. Two friends will meet me at the gym, and then on to my gift, another day of living my life with purpose. I am so thankful. I have laid out my favorite clothes today: a pair of old jeans and a colorful tee shirt. Now off to "wear" my day takes me, into the most beautiful thing called sunlight where the energy of life goes on. I am so grateful, and if you know me you know I love to laugh and enjoy my time. Enjoy yours too; the clock is ticking. I've got things to do, so do you. Get up, get dressed and go out into your world. Remember to "wear" your life bright and beautiful. SHINE ON FRIENDS!!!

ROSES BLOOMING

I have some wonderful pictures of my life that I keep in an old shoe box. It's amazing to look at some of those old pics and think of the times I have been blessed to have with family and friends, but I don't really look at them often because today is what life is really is all about. You can lose sight of today when you get stuck in the past. I know what has been, but I don't want to be a "has-been." Memories are fantastic, like taking a train ride and looking out the back window. I'd rather look forward to where I'm going.

I brought an old picture of myself to show a friend, and the friend said, "Oh my goodness, is that you?" I said, "Now look at me." "Oh my, it is you." Hope you see who I am today and just say, "My, how you have bloomed!"

Remember, a rose bud preparing to bloom can be a pretty sight but oh, when the flower comes into its exquisite beauty it is breathtaking! Let your beauty SHINE in this moment called a day!!!

A DAY AT THE FAIR

Life can be like a day at the fair: early excitement and anticipation on what one can see and do because there are so many things going on around us such as distractions and options. I think we lose sight of our direction at times, and then we take everything for granted.

Life on the midway...I know I have written this several times, but life is moving very quickly for me in my senior years. I am trying, carefully, to take in all the sights and sounds so I do not take one minute for granted. Last night as I walked my dog just before dark, I noticed the skies behind my home. Silver blue streaks with white shades, reminding me of the favorite marble I had when I was a young boy. I loved playing marbles on the dirt road in front of our house. It was a thousand years ago, it seems. Right now, I am listening to the sounds of nightfall. The wind is giving music to the leaves in the big oak. We can be so caught up in what will be tomorrow that we fail to enjoy that which is today - this hour, this minute, and this gift called life. In the past I have been so anxious to get to where I need to be, but THIS IS WHERE I NEED TO BE right now. Dear GOD, I enjoy now, for whatever is; I let go of whatever is not; and I appreciate this ride I'm on. My fingers are no longer nimble, casing mail for so many years has done a number on them. I think some people might suspect that I've lost my marbles sometimes. There is still a little kid inside of me wanting to have some fun. True, there are some rides at the fair I don't think I want to go on. However, I am going to enjoy my walk down the midway, friends. I hope you will too. Every day is a day to SHINE!!!

STAR MATERIAL

When I was a young boy, before the bullying started in school and before I "had" to conform to the norm, I already knew that I did not fit into the mold of what most people thought a little boy should be and act like. Take, for instance, when I used to go around to neighbors' houses and sing. Yes, sing. Most would say to me, "Stevie, I think I hear your mother calling you." Well, I mean, you can't win them all. One nice, older lady would clap and give me a piece of candy. You hear all the down effects of growing up and there is a list, but kids, I'm going to make the best of it. Good news, I'm back to singing again and the critics are back too. Some birds will never be seen in this neck of the woods again.

The point is, BE WHO YOU ARE and be good at it. When we are young, we want to be like everyone else.

Don't be like the cookie cutter neighborhood where almost every house is the same color with the same plants and [gulp] even have the same mailboxes. Not for me, they would kick me out of the neighborhood in a flash. And, while I'm on this roll, when you get to the age where you don't care what someone else thinks about you...it's heaven! Whatever period of LIFE you are in, SHINE like never before. Hey, if this is my closing act, I'm gonna give it everything I've got before the curtain goes down! Now, take that wonderful act called "you" on the road and fill those seats. You never know who might be in the audience. If only vaudeville would come back...have I got a number in mind. Enjoy your day and delight in being YOU because you are awesome! You are star material, and do not forget, I'm your agent, ten percent baby. Now SHINE!!!

WHO ARE YOU?

There is so much freedom in knowing who you really are without seeking approval from anyone. Who YOU are has nothing to do with what you look like or where you came from. Our spirit is cocooned in our body, this life form, and those who cannot see or choose not to make the effort usually don't venture beyond what the eyes show them. Sadly, many miss the true message.

People, it's the SOUL that lies within each of us that truly carries our purpose. My earthly eyes are fading, but my spiritual eyes are seeing things that I never noticed before. Layers of truth are shedding before me. Indeed, we are subject to the physical form but so few of us go beyond. It's like a great light has been turned on. Everything we touch and everything we see in this dimension is really only a mirage, like the set of a play or movie, and it will all be torn down one day when the purpose is over. But what lies in the soul - the heart of the person - will be eternal. Dear friends, when you look at each other, try to go beyond what you see and look with LOVE upon the soul within.

Someone recently accused me of being gullible, an easy target. Perhaps I am naive. It's alright, no problem. I understand and do not seek approval, do not need it. I am ME, being ME, and honestly having a good time at it. I hope the same for each and every one of you. Look beyond because that is where we are all heading...SHINE!!!

REAL ESTATE

Happiness is like real estate: "It's all about location, baby." There is nothing in the world like happiness. It's what we all desire, and "let it come from inside you." There are many obstacles to having a perfect life...the perfect mate, perfect children, perfect house, perfect job, need I go on? But "perfect" is one tough customer. Someone said to me, "You shouldn't have to work at being happy." Well, I think it does require some work; there is no better tool than being grateful, grateful for what is in your life rather than lament over what is not. Have appreciation for all the blessings God has showered on you.

Often, we watch television shows about people in search of their dream house. Most of the time, I am amazed at all the requirements on the checklist (in order to make them happy): these floors and those walls and this and that and a price tag that makes me gulp. For a second, I think, *why don't I have that?* Then I realize "all this" is really only on loan. Someday, someone else will be in possession of everything I now call mine. So why not find happiness in what there is, who you are and all that is in your heart? Thank you, God! One grateful resident here, my friend. And I like my address, a street paved with happiness and a sign outside front that reads OPEN HEART. Be happy friends and SHINE in the life you have!!!

LIFE IS A BUFFET

Some people claim that they have been inspired to greatness by famous people: actors, star athletics, politicians, etc. I was inspired by a server at a restaurant. True story here. I was in my late teens or maybe early twenties when I went into a buffet style diner where you slide an empty tray along an assembly line and chose which varieties of food you wanted to put on your plate. There were servers along the way to place the food you chose on your plate. Most of them had sedate expressions – nice, even - but you knew to them it was just a job. Then I came to him...a young black man who had a smile as big as Texas and bright as the afternoon sun. He was singing, laughing and appeared to be very kind. This happy–go-lucky guy made you want to enjoy a simple item like string beans, as if they were the only item on the menu. He was beaming as he performed this simple job and was making it into something beautiful. I could *feel* his warm and caring attitude. This young man was my hero, so much so that I decided right then and there I wanted to be just like him! It has become my life's work.

Sometimes life can be mundane, boring and predictable. How many times have we gone to work - at whatever we do - and wish that we were somewhere else? I understand that, but I will stand on this: when you work, work for the glory of GOD, and whatever it is that you do, it is important and will make a difference in our world.

Dear friends, we live in a world full of cameras today; everyone is watching you and somewhere out there might be someone like me and you will have a chance to be a role model. Smile, laugh, and care about everyone you might serve or encounter. That young man did not know it, but he changed my entire outlook on life. He taught me to SHINE. NOW, go out and do the same. Don't forget, life is like a buffet, so much to choose from. Sprinkle some love and care on your plate! Make your life taste good...SHINE!!!

A WINNING HAND

One of my friends is a truly skilled bridge player. He and his wife have won several tournaments. Heck, I struggle at Rummy and Old Maid! I guess it's all in how you play your cards, similar to life. Some people are handed some pretty tough "cards" at birth, born with challenges from day one. Heredity can definitely play a part or just plain being born in the wrong place.

Let's talk heredity. There is a long line of bald-headed men smiling down on me in my family tree, and although I was born on the wrong side of the tracks, there were also wonderful cards stacked in the deck - loving parents and a beautiful family to complete the match. In today's world they want to make everything level and fair, but friends it will never, ever, be level or fair. My best advice to anyone...work hard at making your life a success regardless of your beginning, what's been given to you by life or where you've been placed. It's up to you; shuffle those cards to your advantage, pay attention to what you have in your hand. Make it a winning hand! There are aces in every deck. No excuses, sorry (forget about the jokers). If you want it, work for it...it *can* be done. I am an extremely social person, but I don't care for socialism. I have had many jobs of all kinds and I have the hands of a working man, proud of it, too! I have worked very hard and blessed to have everything I have. As for playing cards, my sister can tell you when I've got a winning hand you can tell 'cause I'm singing, it's a given. As I look at the life I've had, you know it - I am singing all the time! Hope you will too. No matter what cards are placed in your hand, play them gracefully and you will always be a winner. Have a great day and SHINE!!!

LIFE IS NOT ALWAYS A PIECE OF CAKE

"No pain, no gain." That is a very well-known saying for those of us who spend a lot of time in the gym, and may I add it is also for those of us who have spent a lot of time on earth. No denying it, pain comes with the territory. For me it's been like the food I was told was good for me, but I could not stand to eat. My mother put it on my plate and told me if I wanted dessert (the good stuff) I better clean my plate first.

Truly, dear friends, I've had to clean my plate with perseverance many times in my life in order to "get the good stuff." I think WE all have at one time or the other. It can't be avoided. Pain and sorrow are on the menu. I can't say - I won't say - that is has been good for me or anyone else, but I suppose it's all in the taking. You can let it kill you or it can make you stronger. I am a sensitive person, and happen to be male, that alone caused me a great deal of pain. Boys in my day were not allowed to show that HUMAN side of them. Some idiot somewhere decided that being a male meant you could never cry or be vulnerable. Many times, I was pushed around and bullied. It made me strong, and eventually the pain brought the gain. I am not the only one who has experienced this pain. I'm sure each and every one of you can say you have experienced situations in your own life that brought you pain, heartache and sorrow. It's part of life and a part of the problem in the world. Someone must be held responsible for the pain and might very well be if not in this world, then in the next. But it's still up to you to choose how you are going to deal with it. We are responsible for how we treat our fellow human beings in this life. You may not see it, but your neighbor, your friend, the person you walk by might be dealing with their own personal pain.

Remember that when you deal with them. Take your pain and use it for good. Gain insight on understanding so you can pay it forward.

Living life is not a piece of CAKE. Sometimes there are things your plate that you need to digest before you proceed. Be careful how you size someone up; have mercy, show love and acquire insight from everything on your own plate. If we can learn from the past, the future will taste *soooooooo* good! Please pass me some kindness and I will pass you some love! Wishing each and every one of you an awesome day...SHINE!!!

FATHER'S DAY

Happy Father's Day! My father was, I believe, the kindest man I will ever meet in my life, hands down. Never, ever, did I hear say anything bad about anyone. He was easygoing and a person who never wanted anything to change, unlike myself who has always welcomed change. Dad lived in the same house for most of his life, worked at the same business most of his life, and rarely questioned life, itself. He believed in simplicity and he often told me, if given the chance, he would live his entire life over, entirely the same way. I give him a glowing 5-star review as a father. One day, I hope my children can say the same. I believe a child is the ultimate gift from GOD, for GOD is allowing you the ultimate gift of raising and caring for His most divine creation, LIFE. You can make mistakes in your life - I have made some - but at the end of the day, never make the mistake of ignoring your child. My children knew I loved them. I was a hands-on father when I got home from work when they were young. It WAS all about them. Would I make changes in the way I raised them? Some. I've grown a lot since then, learned a lot since then, but those were some of the best days of my life! Nothing is worth more than a child, nothing. Most men can father a child, but it takes a special man to be a father. Thank you, GOD, for the opportunity. It was one I would never have wanted to miss out on. My love for storytelling has always been with me and when they were young, after their bath time they were tucked into bed and I would read to them, often in my work uniform. I would lie down on the carpet in their room and read a short book and then make up my own story. Sometimes I would fall asleep and wake up about two in the morning, still in my uniform, wondering who I was and where I was.

Then off to shower and back into my own bed. Nevertheless, they got their stories and now, you are too. See, life does go on and I'm still in the business of storytelling. "Night-night children," like I would tell them. "Dad's a million years tired; off to bed for me." Dream on and SHINE!!!

MIRROR, MIRROR ON THE WALL

The gym world is a very important place to me; it has become part of my life. Some years are better than others. Let's face it, everything gets tougher with age. Needing to keep those leg muscles in shape is an uphill battle. One thing every gym has in common is mirrors everywhere. The late Mae West was asked why she had a mirror on her ceiling and her reply was, "To see how I'm doing." Some men can be just as vain creatures as some woman are, believe it or not. Everyone wants to look their "best." A trip to a gym is all it takes to realize you are not there yet, not even close. How many of us live our lives comparing ourselves to others? Joe is stronger, Jim has the better career, Mary has the prettiest hair etc.

Life can be like going to an audition, there is a lot of competition in the line. I say remember to flash a big smile. Enjoy being you and don't depend on the mirror to see how you're doing. Let it come from the heart. Be good to yourself because there will always be the greater and the lesser. Know your part; do it well and give yourself a pat on the shoulder. Have a great day, love the person in the mirror 'cause if you do, I guarantee you will SHINE!!!

YOUNG AT HEART

Oh, to be a kid again! Summer is coming and what beautiful childhood memories of when a Slip and Slide meant fun, not having an accident on the floor. And Crystal Rocks were something you put in water, not something you smoked. Back then, collecting bottle caps got you in the fun show and for us "poor" kids, running in and out of a plastic sprinkler was more fun than a barrel of monkeys. It was a time when your dad let you bring the neighbor kids to the drive-in movie in his station wagon. And your mom would give the OK to fill the back of the car with blankets and pillows. Today, many people recommend that you eat organic food. Back then I would eat [cheap] raw hot dogs and drink from a hose hooked up to our well-water and stay up late to watch "Creature Feature."

Maybe I am just an old man, but I think children today are missing out on really having fun; so many of them are always in the house by choice. We used to get up and head out the front door to do things - simple things - like building a tree fort in our front yard. Today the homeowner's board would send you a certified letter slapped with a big fine! But man, those were the best days! Of course, our parents thought so too. Have a good day, KIDS, play nice and get home before dark! Keep in mind, there's always tomorrow to SHINE!!!

SHINE YOUR LOVE LIGHT BRIGHT

Those of us who are believers know the greatest second commandment is to love thy neighbor as thyself and at times, this can be a toughie. Just looking for a parking spot tries your patience in the quest. See how easily you can be put to the test? Every day can be a challenge whether small or large.

It was like any other day as I passed by a young man and told him to have a good day. His immediate reaction was, "Why did you say that?" People can be suspicious of kindness in itself. The world is getting darker; we believers need to "Keep Your love Light Shining" bright to show the way. No one ever said it would be easy. I grew up in the sixties when the hippie movement set out on a mission to bring forth love not war. Their great logo was the peace symbol. Sorry, it didn't work, kids.

The reality is plain and simple: there will never be absolute peace on this planet, never. You can enforce every law there is and there will still be an apple, still be a snake in the garden.

Okay, what are our options? Move to the top of a mountain and hide in a cave? Many moments I've had that very thought. But how can I live out my purpose doing my part to let GOD'S love shine through me if I check out of society? Do you doubt that GOD chose you to represent Him? I don't. When you love your fellow man, you honor the Creator who made the heavens and the earth. Show respect for his creation. Sometimes it is a tedious task. We have all failed one time or another, but we are still on his payroll. He hasn't fired me yet.

Outside, in our world, it can be a dark, dark place. But if you keep the "light" on, you can help others find the path. When you love your neighbor, you are loving your Creator. Choose love, have a great morning, friends. Let it shine, let it shine, let it SHINE!!!

TICKING ALONG

This is a repeat, but a knock-out gem. Here's today's quote to go along with it: "DON'T LET TIME DECIDE HOW YOUR LIFE WILL BE LIVED," rather "LIVE YOUR LIFE WITH GUSTO IN WHAT TIME THERE IS." Decide to delight in what time there is and adjust to the moving hands of the clock. The secret is to keep ticking along.

Can't believe it's halfway through 2019. I'm up and ready for the day, don't want to waste a second. My partner-in-crime, my little dog, is up too. Nobody has to tell her, she knows it's chow time. And, she never misses a beat...tick, tick, tick. It's time to SHINE, everyone!!!

INNER VOICES

Have you ever been in a restaurant with friends and it's so noisy that you can't hear what's being said? I think our lives can be much like that. There are so many distractions around us that we don't listen to our inner voice. It's there, the secret is to listen. I think it's something really, really important that we just overlook. I'm working on it ever so carefully. Funny, it's been there all along and yet I've never appreciated it. Trust yourself. Listen because WHO you are is the most valuable gift you have to offer the world. Really, deep inside you is everything, every tool you need to get the job done. Work on you, 'cause YOU SHINE!!!

SPICE IT UP

If something on your plate of Life is hard to swallow, "add some flavor and put a little spice in it." For most of us, everyday life can become, at times, a task instead of an adventure, a job in itself that can sometimes be a boring routine. I say hide some treats and indulge once and a while because as you have probably heard, a spoonful of sugar helps the medicine go down. When you take care of yourself, you take care of everyone in your path. I always have a little jar of this or a bottle of that to enhance the flavor of my food. "Spice it up kids, bon appétit!" Now go out and find some something fun to do! I know I will. Whatever you do make sure you SHINE!!!

COURAGE CALLED YOUR NAME

To all the young men who made the sacrifice and gave their lives so that we may live in a free country: We have not forgotten your extreme sacrifice! For most of you, many, many years have passed...and you sleep on. So many dreams you dreamed...gone. How many suns have come up, how many moons have passed since that dawn...and you sleep on? What could have been was not for you when you choose to fight. Mothers, fathers and sweethearts cried when they were notified that you died...and you sleep on. Courage called your name and you met the call. Peace and safety for all...and you sleep on.

Young men, we have not forgotten that because of your bravery, the flag will stand and fly. We could not say goodbye. Until we meet again, the days will pass and there will be a midnight and a dawn...and you sleep on. We will remember all of you with well earned respect. This is dedicated to all our fallen heroes. They "SHINE" in the heavens above.

THROUGH THE EYES OF A CHILD

I was reading that a famous movie star of 65 announced to the world that he is now dating a 20-something year old young woman and proud of it. So good for him, and good for her, and so on. Personally, I would feel awkward. I mean, just imagine discussing my favorite music from the past and the bands I use to listen to, or my favorite cartoons or cars. I could go on but to tell you the truth, I have shoes older than her. But he is super rich [ahh, come on, you know it helps] and super famous, and also in great shape for a man of his age.

Which brings me to my own story: he and I are close in age, we both work out, we both go to the gym, we watch what we eat and we are both trying to keep it all together. I'm neither rich nor famous but I too am in the up and coming geezer club. Sometimes we get reminded like it or not.

Not too long ago, my wife was watching a friend's young child and she was reading to him. I was in the kitchen cleaning up and trying to be quiet so I would not disturb them. Later, the little boy asked my wife, "Are you married?" She said yes and told him, "The man that you saw in the kitchen is my husband." The boy replied, "Oh, that old man I saw cleaning?" I laughed till I cried because that young boy saw me through young eyes and what he said kept me ever so humble. To each his own.

I wish that famous guy good times with his young chick. I'll stick to what I know, someone who remembers how to dial a rotary phone and remembers that Captain Kangaroo was on television and not at a zoo. Have a great day everyone, and SHINE!!!

A LETTER TO MY SON

No one, including me, likes to talk about death, but nevertheless, death is very much a part of Life. We were a young couple with a young child and one day we received good news, our son would have a sibling. The perfect picture, a "Leave it to Beaver" world, and everything would be beautiful.

One day my wife came home from what I thought would be a routine doctor's visit, but she was crying. The news was that our child had a rare condition. I truly cannot remember the name, but the internal organs were not developing correctly, and we were advised to have an abortion. We decided to go by faith and move forward. I can tell you it was a strange feeling because life went on as usual. The sun came up, people laughed while our world was colored in gray tones. We did our best to move ahead, but I can tell you, my mind raced with scary thoughts. What if the child had severe needs, could we cope? Would I be able to afford the medical bills? It was a tough, tough time.

One day I came home, and my wife was in pain; her legs were swollen so we rushed to the hospital. After she was assessed, we were told that her body was shutting down due to toxins. Soon, our son came into the world without a cry. We were placed in the maternity ward where new life was all around us...and our child was gone. They told me if I wanted, they could dispose of my child's body, but I preferred to give this precious little boy a proper burial. That night, I went home and wrote him a letter. It may sound silly, his soul was already gone, but I wanted him to know that he was wanted, and that his mom and dad loved him very much. We did; we still do. I often wonder what he would have looked like. It's been over thirty years now, so he'd be a grown man. No one talks about him, but I do. There is nothing, nothing worth more than a child in my book. I see all these smirk politicians and famous celebrities discussing abortions like it's a trip to the dentist and my heart goes out to every woman who has ever had an abortion and to every couple who has lost a child because I'm sure the thought comes forth of what might have been, if only.

Someday, after my work here is done, I expect to go beyond the skies and a very handsome young man will meet me with an old, weathered letter in his hand. I know I will recognize him, my boy! I'll probably say, "Well kid, your pop finally made it. What have you been up to?" It will be a golden time moment and every tear will be wiped away. As I wrote, I don't like to talk about death but it's everywhere. Still, LIFE goes on and I plan to as long as GOD plans me to do so.

Yeah, I've cried a lot, but I laughed a lot too. One of my favorite sayings is "I've got fields to plow." I do. And I better get to them. Gray days do come, but ah, the power of sunshine generates life. It can shine form the outside and from the inside, it is so BEAUTIFUL! Come on everybody, let's SHINE!!!

ROSE COLORED GLASSES

The other day I visited a local shoppe and was talking with a bright young lady. And like I've said, there are no subjects I'm not willing to discuss. We talked about the democratic debates going on this week. Let's just say that we see things differently. Nevertheless, I found her bright, interesting and aware of the world around her. And I see hope for future generations. My own generation came forth at a pivotal period in time. Change was in the air. Thoughts, music and images were becoming controversial. I remember my parents being in shock over the popularity of the Beatles, the long hair and the acceptance of smoking pot. We had not yet come into the computer age, but new inventions were knocking on our doors. Life would never be the same, but will it?

The other day a young mother had her child in the seat of a shopping basket and when it came time to pay, this young child tried to put the payment card into the machine - something that so many of us older folks struggle with. I marvel, change it is a coming again. Every human emotion is still evident...love, hate, happiness, sorrow and the world still turns; it will go on. The young woman and I were polite to each other and I asked her about her future plans. I am excited for her and hope she does well. I can remember thinking back then that I knew so much more than my parents did. Now that I have had a long run at this business of life, I will tell you in hindsight that I knew very little about life. I'm in my sixties, and still do not have a clue. The classroom never ends, but I want to continue to learn and I am thankful for everything my parents taught me. I feel like I have a responsibility for being citizen of this planet and I am concerned about where this world is going. There is a new group of players here, a new generation filled with new kids on the block. I listen to the young people and I am careful not to pass any judgment, only advise them if they want it. After all, I was once up to bat but now I'm in the out, outfield. Things sure do look different this far out, don't they? Someone get my glasses, please; it's all how you look at it, so SHINE EVERYONE!!!

BEHIND THE SCENES

Outside of my porch there is a bird's nest with three babies. I was going to send out birth announcements because for me it is a happy event. The babies are chirping fiercely as they wait impatiently for their mother to feed them. Mother bird is flying to and fro to scavenging for earthworms to feed to her chicks. Poor Mom, no time to rest, but she is doing her part to keep the universe going, as we all must.

Have you ever thought about the importance of doing what needs to be done, both great and small in your daily life? We often live in a Hollywood world where awards are given out to the beautiful people. Yet, someone has to clean the dishes when the banquet is over right? There are so many unsung heroes out in our world that never get recognition. Unfortunately, they just get passed over and sadly take for granted. These heroes are often in the shadows or in the backstage of the production. Applause ignites as the star steps out on the stage. But somewhere behind the scenes a person or team exists that paved the runway to help the star shine.

I will never ever forget an elderly woman who lived on one of my postal routes. She would often write little notes thanking me for my service to her. One time she told me that I was in her prayers and that one day I'd know that. I felt blessed by her acknowledgment. When someone appreciates what you do for them, it really makes all the difference in the world. I try to do the same and let those who serve me know that I am grateful. "Thank you, I appreciate you." Those simple words can make a world of difference to the people doing the things they have to do. We can't all be famous, but let's be "famous" for what we do when we acknowledge the people in our lives who do what needs to be done, great and small regardless of any recognition they might receive. They are the wind beneath your wings.

Can't wait till the babies start to fly away 'cause I need to trim the bush they are nesting in...'cause that's what I do. Peep-peep, chirp-chirp...have a good day doing what you enjoy. And shine while you are doing it...SHINE!!!

TAKE-OFF PAD

Remember when I wrote about the bird's nest in my garden? Here's the update for everyone who's interested to know. The babies are now out of the nest and up and about. From my patio I can hear their distinctive sounds above all the other bird noise. I see the mother flying around and keeping an eye on them. I believe that GOD is very, very much like that. He knows the sounds of those He created, which is all of mankind, and we need to call out to Him because He is keeping an eye on us. I don't use elaborate words or set a certain time to speak with GOD. For me it's an ongoing conversation. Sometimes, I guess, like those little birds might be doing, I am chirping for "help" and often chirping for strength to get through a rough day. You may think you're as tough as a street fighter, but when it all comes down to brass tacks, "You ain't nothing" without GOD! Remember, LIFE can be one big garden and there are a lot of beautiful things out there, but some scary things also. Spread your wings and fly, just keep in contact with the flight tower, aka God. Ready, set, time for "take-off!" Have a great day and as always...SHINE!!!

KEEP YOUR SOUL IN CHECK

Isn't the creation of a human being fascinating, complex, extraordinarily amazing and unique? I witnessed the birth of my children and from early on realized that they arrived with their own little personalities. Even though they were raised by the same parents in the same environment, they all possess different traits. You can look at them and see some visual connection, but their souls are each one of a kind. I don't know how personalities are created in the soul. In an abstract view, I almost see a blender with several ingredients being mixed about and poured into the flesh, and then events and situations come into play and after nine months of being cocooned, a baby emerges. Then comes life's schooling and the soul is put into training. We are taught who to love, who to hate and what is right or wrong.

Nothing makes me sadder than when I see certain groups teach their children to hate someone because they look different or believe different. I, personally, can't think of a worse sin than to take an innocent mind and teach it to hate. How many factories of hate machines are out there in our world? That is why it is very important to "Keep the SOUL in check." The soul is the essence of WHO you really are, believe it or not. Each of us has a responsibility for our own lives, but we also have a responsibility for lives of others. Licenses are given for all kinds of things: driving a car, running a business, hunting, flying and many important tasks declaring that you have been properly trained to operate correctly. And you've been given a SOUL as well, a unique one-of-a-kind creation. Value it, guard it, guide it...for the good of everything, everybody and with the greatest command given by the Creator: "Love one another as I have loved you." Shine everyone, SHINE!!!

VALUABLE PIECES OF ART

Today I watched a show about someone who had a very valuable piece of art in their house for years and never realized it. I think so many of us are much like that. We have God-given talents within ourselves and never, ever use them. We behave as though we are so poor, yet we are rich beyond our imagination. ASK AND YOU SHALL RECEIVE, LOOK WITHIN FOR IT WAS THERE ALL ALONG. SHINE!!!

FIELD OF BROKEN DREAMS

My sister came to stay with me for a couple of days and we went to visit our late uncle's grave to pay our respects. It has been several years since we were both there and, for me, it puts a whole new perspective on my life, one that I do not take for granted. The cemetery looks like an ancient land devoid of grass. There are headstones and markers scattered everywhere. But because there was no office, we took to memory searching for his grave. My shadow moved across the land on this bright sunny day, but it was filled with sorrow. I came across the grave of a young child, born the same year that I was, yet he only lived to the age of eleven. Fifty-two years later, here I am. I cannot tell you why I am here on earth alive and this young precious child was only given such a short time a short purpose to live. But I am certain there has to be a reason, and I remind myself that life is certainly a most precious gift.

I believe that there is divine reason for the time we are given. Perhaps a chance meeting with a stranger will have a significant effect on your own history. Maybe your purpose might be to help someone through a crisis. I don't know and don't come close to knowing...but it's there, I'm here, and for whatever reason I've been blessed with a long run. I want to do well with it and use whatever time I have wisely.

Back to the beginning. We finally found our uncle and aunt's graves, side by side as they had been in life. We bowed our heads and said a prayer. In so many ways it was a prayer of thanksgiving. They lived right next store to our family of six. Unfortunately, life had not blessed them with children of their own. Our parents did not have much money so our uncle and aunt always made an effort to make our lives special.

On holidays, our aunt would come running over to our house and shower us with extra gifts. They had played an important part in our lives. So, when we walked away into the bright sunlight, past the fields of broken dreams, a place where grief has an eternal hold, a place where time has stopped for many, we walked on to living our lives as usual. A place busy with moving pieces and spinning energies, a place where there is still a clock ticking.

Seize the day my friends, every second is important. Make good on your purpose to do good; love one another. Cast your shadows wisely and SHINE!!!

THE WINDS OF TIME

Over the last few years, perhaps from becoming older, I have become aware of one of our most precious gifts...TIME. Another day to get it right. I rejoice in it. I do not dwell on my past, but I am aware of some mistakes I have made. Sometimes it's not *what* you say but the *way* you say it, and if I hurt someone with careless words, I repent...even to those who harmed me first and I reacted back, retaliated. How they dealt with me was their business. I know that I am responsible for my own actions.

If we are to grow as human beings, the first action is to take responsibility for what we do and say and how we live. I own who I am; no one else is to blame. I have an urge to amend and if I can and say I'm sorry if I ever did anything to hurt our relationship. I desire to move on toward the light of a new day filled with anticipation for love and joy. I really want to like the person I have become.

Friends, we ALL have lessons to learn, so learn them. Value every human and animal life on the planet.

It is dark now outside my window, but soon, - very, very soon - the precious gift of another day will arrive. Light will come with it and my heart soars with all the possibilities that also come with it. I want to be ready for it. The winds of time are in the air. Breathe deeply and exhale. Wake up in the morning sun and SHINE!!!

TRY TO FIND THE GOOD IN PEOPLE

You might think I'd run out of things to write [talk] about but not a chance! A good friend of mine once pinned a nickname on me, "Motor-mouth." She was right on, but really it's just that I am curious about life and people - all kinds of people - and what makes them tick. I like diversity. I find it sad that some people dismiss others because they march to the beat of a different drum. You might miss out on finding a good friend, a unique friend, a life-long friend. Do you realize how quickly some people can label someone crazy? Well, being a little crazy can be fun to me.

Annie (true story with pseudonym) was a customer of mine years and years ago. To be honest, at first I found her a touch frightening. She had a wild mane of hair with eyes to match and a laugh that would come from deep within her large body that would vibrate like a megaphone. Annie loved animals. She told me she could talk with them and even understand what they said back. And although, as she told me, "I don't own them, they are free to come and go as they want," everything from snakes to dogs and anything that could fly would all hang with Annie. One day she asked me if I'd like to meet Oscar [I think that was the name] so I said "sure" and before I knew it, she slung this creature around my neck. I wanted to scream! It was an old weather-beaten ferret. She looked me straight in the eyes and told me that he approved of me [just what I was hoping for]. Annie was as the saying goes "poor as a church mouse." Her house was run down big time, but she was rich with love for animals, creatures and the life she had, never, ever a complaint. Years later I met her nephew in a local convenience store, and I asked about her. I was profoundly sad when he told me that she had taken her own life because the city was going to condemn her house, take all the animals away, and place her in a housing center. It broke my heart because she was my friend and I loved her.

If you follow my posts, you know I've written about a black snake that lives in my garden. I don't like snakes at all, but I say, "live and let live." We share everything but the property taxes as I have told you before. But when I think of my wonderful friend, I know she would have loved that snake. Do I talk to my snake? Yes. But remember, a little crazy can be fun. Have a great day my friends and try to find something good about everyone...try, that's all I'm asking. I am a little crazy, but proud of it too! SHINE!!!

A LIFE-LONG CONTRACT

You might come to realize by now that I don't hold back from discussing any subject, friends. I believe that dialog is the best remedy to find a common ground in any situation. One's faith, one's religious belief, is a very personal arena and a place where total respect must be established. Still, there are times where things need to be brought out in the open. Some years ago, someone I love very much decided to leave a church that our family had been a member of for generations. She found peace and a solid foundation for her spiritual walk someplace else. Not everyone shared her joy and enthusiasm. Someone that she had gone to high school with, and once a close friend, abandoned their friendship. This "best pal" will no longer talk with her. The friendship is over, finis, persona non gratis.

Though it was not me who received the "pink-slip" on friendship, it hurt me to witness this act. I suppose most of us have an idea what GOD is like and what He expects.

My own personal teachings about God in my early years brought fear. I thought He was this ancient man who resembled the character Moses, much like the late actor Charlton Heston played in "The Ten Commandments" and at any moment a lightning bolt could strike me down. I'm still here, but I will say I don't know what God looks like or what GOD is really like, but I DO believe he is the greatest author ever. He's already read my book from cover to cover and he knows every single flaw I possess. And still...He loves me. I don't think he will ever give me the "pink slip"...it's a life-long contract. If I stay authentic to my creation mixed with all the ingredients, human and spiritual [sometimes at war with each other], everything will be alright. Especially if I cover it in LOVE for my fellow man. LOVE, above everything else, will guide us through this journey. If LOVE is not there, you cannot survive because it is everything. Sounds silly, child-like, perhaps dribble? I can understand, but LOVE is the key to all understanding and personal growth. It was right there all along, inside each of us, like the ruby slippers Dorothy wore. LOVE will guide you home if you let it. You are not called to understand how faith works for another. What you are called for is to love your fellow man.

Have a wonderful Sunday and enjoy each other and all the things GOD has created us for. One of my favorite attractions at the "happiest place on earth" has a song. "It Really Is a Small Word After All" filled with all kinds of people, with all kinds of beliefs, under one heaven. Let's enjoy the ride together. After all, it goes by fast, doesn't it? SHINE EVERYONE!!!

THE FABRICS OF OUR LIVES

If you asked me what I think is one of the greatest qualities I look for in a friend, one would be loyalty. Nothing is better than knowing someone loves you despite knowing all your flaws. Cannot deny it friends, we are a flawed bunch. Second, would be a sense of humor. I love to laugh, including at myself. Sometimes we take ourselves too seriously and think we are the center of the universe. It's like going to my gym where there are mirrors everywhere, so you can't avoid who you see...who you are. At times we like what we see, other times we'd rather edit the picture. The good thing, for me, is that I've come to terms. I don't need to promote the man in the mirror, just simply enjoy him. I can be ridiculous at times - singing out loud, a little dance or two - but let me put it this way...it's time to take the plastic off the fabric [me] and enjoy the moment.

My father and mother once owned a car with a top-notch fabric interior, and they had plastic put over it to preserve the beauty. I hated it. Can you imagine plastic in the hot Florida sun? Burns your butt off when you try to sit down on it. Years later, they put the car up for sale and took the plastic off. Yes, the seats were still beautiful. But think about it, we could have enjoyed the pleasure of the fabric all those years. This guy is going to enjoy the fabric of my life while I can and find some laughter in the moments. I went to the gym one day and started working out when a friend took me aside and I believe he said that I had my shirt inside out. As a young man, I would have been mortified and embarrassed. That day I laughed so hard I cried. My plastic is off, and it feels soooooooooooooooooo good.

Have some fun and sprinkle some laughter in your day...SHINE!!!

SENIOR CITIZEN DISCOUNTS

Here we go again. I've told this story before but it's good enough to make a comeback! I went into a place of business and there was a young, pretty woman behind the counter, and she said, "Wow, you're in good shape, aren't you?" And I thought, *man, I still have what it takes!!!* But before I could enjoy the moment, she quickly answered back, "For a man of YOUR age!" Talk about a balloon busting. Then to top it off she asked, "Are you married?" And before I could reply she said, "Not for me, but my mother is looking for someone!" Ahhh, but I was quicker still. I shot back, "What about Grandma?"

You just gotta laugh. Laughter is good medicine, right? Well I did and it felt good. Look, I can remember at 18 thinking 35 was over the hill and now I think at 63 I'm still climbing. Truth is, I'm on the other side of the mountain and coming down. That is the cycle of life and the way it is supposed to be. The best thing I feel is to keep it going for as long as you can. When I was a young man, older people would complain that this hurts and that hurts and I'd think, "sure," now I'm sure that they were sure, and it sure does! But there are some rewards too. Especially when you say, "Do you honor senior discounts here?" This golden boy is gonna Shine! Come on everybody, it's SHINE TIME!!!

SHINING IN A MOST DIVINE PLACE

Dear friends, today was a sad day for me. I have received the news of the death of a young man in my family. Though we have not been close, as I have moved several times over the years, I knew him when he was a little boy. I grieve for his mother and wonderful grandmother and his sister. Gone way, way too soon. I ponder the story in the Bible when Jesus wept at the death of Lazarus. I don't think Jesus was weeping over his death so much, rather he knew the pain it would leave upon his loved ones. Death is never ever easy, yet it is very much a part of our world. I often think how life goes on after we are gone. The sun will come up, the moon will welcome the night, and the stars will claim the evening skies. Life will go on. When someone we love dies, I don't think we really get over it, we deal with it. We adjust our lives and keep living. A compromise with time is made. When a young person dies, it hits me the hardest because I think of what might have been. The "what might have beens" are the toughest. My faith tells me that GOD, the Author of life, knows all things we do not. Somehow and in someplace though, their essence and light [no longer here] must surely shine in a most divine place. They are in a world where there are no tears, sadness or sorrow; and are complete within the love of GOD. One day we will see them again...whole, complete and just like GOD created them...perfect! I believe...SHINE!!!

THE HEART AND THE SOUL REMEMBER

This week I plan to visit a family friend who is really more like a family member, not by blood but by the heart. Now into her nineties, she resides in a nursing home. She remembers who I am, not always my name but there is a special twinkle in her eyes when she smiles at me. She had worked in the medical profession and it only seems like yesterday when she retired. Time has passed quickly. The nursing facility she is in has caring staff and it is clean and comfortable.

I can remember as a child being somewhat frightened by the elderly. Their hands were so cold, and they seemed lifeless. I don't feel that way now. If you're good at math you will realize how fast the years will come...and will go. Those fortunate enough to survive are keenly aware of the reality. I have some friends who say, "I don't ever want to be so old that I can't take care of myself." Who does? No one wants to surrender their independence and leave give up their homes and lifestyle. I remember my father initially refusing to leave his little home. But sooner or later he had to due to medical problems. It's humbling when you have to rely on someone else. I know because there are times now when I help men walk from the store to their rides. They resist at first. Then I tell them, "Let me help you, I don't want you to fall." Often, I whisper, "I understand" because as I grow closer to surrendering to the aging process, it is a given. I have so much respect for the elderly.

Hopefully today, weather permitting, I will go visit my dear friend. It is a blessing to see the joy on her face when she realizes someone who loves her has come for a visit. The wonderful reflection of time in her eyes is priceless. The body surrenders, but the soul and the heart remember. Love is the one thing time cannot hold prisoner. Friends, when you get the time to spend with you loved ones, do not forget to SHINE!!!!

TWO-WAY RADIO

I see a movement in today's world that really disturbs me. There are groups who attack people because they think differently than them, believe differently than they do, and they go to extreme means to silence them.

Many, many years ago I had a customer - an older man - who lived alone. His wife had died, and when he retired, he decided to move down south. You could tell he was a "people person" because he loved to talk. The problem was, so many of us around him were busy trying to make a buck, so we had little time to talk with him. Well, it was the days before the internet, so [I will call him, Bill] Bill went out and bought himself a two-way radio. I am no expert on them, but it was one that let him talk with people all over the world. Suddenly his world became larger. He was so proud of himself and was having a ball talking to this person and that person and making friends all over the world. I never heard him putting anyone down for anything. He was open to learning and found human diversity a joy. I think he had the right idea.

Sometimes people can open up ideas for you. Though I don't go on a radio, I am a very fortunate man. I live in an age where I can talk to people of all walks of life myself, right here on Facebook land. I have friends from all over the map, friends from different walks of life, different faiths, different views on life and...I like that and I like them. When we all come together, we all add color to our world. And isn't color, in itself, a most precious gift? If it's morning where you are then, good morning! If it's evening, good night. So have a good day or a good night everyone. Signing off, out and over, copy that and SHINE!!!

BE A BRAVE SOLDIER

Sometimes there are lines from a movie that strike a chord with me and lead me to think hard. This movie came from an old, very touching classic. A mother was talking to her daughter who had just returned home from a mental facility where she lived after her nervous breakdown. The mother felt guilty and was questioning the way she raised her daughter. She was wondering if her child's nervous breakdown was her fault. Here are the lines as much as I can remember them. "Wouldn't it be great when we are born if we'd all have guarantees that we would have just the right lives and all be happy? But when we are born, we all just have to take chances." And I do wonder. I believe most parents start out with good intentions.

When my first child was born I remember all the plans, all the ideas and all the dreams on how his life would be "perfect," then life comes along, issues come along, and the once crystal-clear waters become cloudy and murky. Suddenly "perfect" no longer exists. I was fortunate to have wonderful parents, but I could not tell you that my youth was at all perfect. I was not the typical American dream boy. I was awful when I attempted to play sports, and in those days that was how the measure of value was put on a male. Fair or not, that was the score. My academics, on the other hand, were passable but nothing to write home about. It took many years for me to sort out what my redeemable qualities were. Most of us who come into this world are bound to face struggles. Those born with all the qualities for success, happiness, fame and fortune all seemed to be wrapped up together in a perfect bundle. You could spend a lifetime wondering why some are given much, and some are not. After all this time, I cannot answer that question. For me, I am ever so grateful for the opportunity of life, and to have lived this long. Hey, I'm still up for lessons...bring them on. There were no guarantees 63 years ago that a little boy born to two wonderful parents would have the right life and be happy. It was a big gamble, one that paid off big time even with the odds that were there.

Some days at my part-time job, young parents bring their infants through my line. When I look at God's beautiful creation in these tiny bodies and those little eyes look back at me, it is as if the child is scanning my soul, and I whisper softly to the child, "Good luck, and much happiness." So off into the world you go...be a brave little soldier and let your inside and outside amour SHINE!!!

THE CLASSROOM OF LIFE

LIFE IS ONE GREAT BIG CLASSROOM...sometimes we are the students and sometimes we are the teachers. I have learned so much as a letter carrier, it was like college for me and I studied all the courses diligently. My major was in life, but other courses came along...philosophy, death, the study of children growing up. And along the way, I received a degree in the study of hard knocks. Hollywood paints their stars with attention given to who is the sexiest man or woman of the year. These heroes and heroines have to be picture perfect with masculine or shapely physiques. But I have seen heroes in a different light.

There was one elderly woman on my route who was the strongest person I'll ever meet. She was a widow and lived with her small dog. She was a woman of great faith who took care of herself and never complained. In her early nineties, she broke her hip, and while she was in the hospital her beloved dog was run over by a car. Nevertheless, she managed to get physically back on track and kept moving. Then one day she met me at the mailbox with tears in her eyes. She told me that her son, who had come to visit her from time to time, had taken his own life. And still she kept going. I've never met someone with that strength. She was my hero.

Every day that I spend at the gym I see people working out with incredible strength. But strength is not always measured by the size of your external muscles. There is an internal muscle...the heart. And there is the essence of the soul and the strength of our beliefs. If that is not in the mix, we've overlooked the lesson. Have a great day and lift your spirit, and the spirit of everyone around you with the determination to keep moving. We must keep moving...SHINE!!!

JUST ONE ACT OF KINDNESS

A really wonderful thing is about to happen in your life, and it's called a new day! No matter what you did, said or experienced yesterday, it's history and you've been given another chance. Perhaps it's with age that I've become so aware of what I say to someone and how I deal with someone, but it is paramount! Laugh if you will, but I'm even taking time to tell the clerk at the register, "Thank you, I value your service!" Yes, I VALUE their service, from the greatest to the least. Most of my life I've been the least, and I can tell you the least are usually the least noticed. Be the one that appreciates, be the one who let's someone know they count. Everyone needs to be valued. It strikes me as so odd that many politicians are going around shouting about how we need to care about this person or that group, yet they show no respect for anyone that dares to differ from their beliefs or thought processes. You can only grow as a human being when you start acting like one. Respect and appreciate your fellow man REGARDLESS of the situation. I am changing, growing, and seeing so many things I've overlooked.

Well, TODAY is a new day, a new opportunity to start over. Will I slip up here or there? Yes, probably, but I'm raising my awareness. Today is a precious gift, my friends, so unwrap it carefully and use the time to become the best YOU that you can be. Share it...respect and appreciation with EVERYONE you see, talk and come in contact with because your one act of kindness might just be a history-breaking event...SHINE!!! EXPECT GREAT THINGS TO HAPPEN!!! Great news...I'M EXPECTING!! No, no, not that. I'm expecting to have a great Thursday. Many times in my life when things went right, I was waiting for the "other shoe to fall." It was the classic "Sword of Damocles," fear of something bad happening after achieving good fortune or success. Maybe you have been like that at times. Have you ever heard someone say, "that's just my luck" or "that's the way my life goes!" Have we trained ourselves to be suspicious of good times, good fortune and great things happening to us? It's not to say there will not be obstacles in our path or difficult situations, but I do believe you need to meditate and prepare your mind to accept that good things are going to happen today. Appreciate the beauty in each day, and open up for opportunities to fill your life with love and try to overcome whatever is standing in your way. Stop asking, "Why is it always me?" Retaliate with, "Thank you God for all that has been given to me," and great things will happen. Expect it, share it, and you will find yourself SHINING!!!

SHIFTING GEARS

When I was younger, many times I had to drive some old jalopies. One was an old truck that had problems shifting into different gears. You could get stuck into a gear and it would be difficult moving forward, much like our lives at times.

I've always been curious about astrology. I've read about the twelve signs regarding our birth months. Some people believe you have chosen your life before you were born but if this is true...what I was thinking?

Mine has been a life struggling to understand so many things. To tell you the truth, I have had quite a few obstacles along the way, but then, maybe most of us do. I remember in my early years in school being around the boys who were good at everything, especially sports. It seemed to me that they had all the right tools and body parts to be successful. And I was a mess, a washout, a skinny little kid who wasn't very coordinated. Even today, we see the super successful athletes reaping all the benefits with their God-given talents. So, the why question pops into my head. Why didn't I have it, all in gear? Now I look at it all in a different light these days. I believe it's not all about what you are given but rather what you do with what you have. I am more than convinced ALL OF US have gifts placed inside of us, rare and wonderful makings of special talent; but we have to seek it out, tune it up, understand it and USE it. Sometimes we are lazy, and we don't want to take the time to explore the inner aspects of our minds, stirrings that could reveal the hidden dimensions of our soul. And then there is sin; yes, I wrote sin. If we fall into a pit of pity and sin, our actions can prevent us from finding our true path. You have, I have, we all have the tools to create and enjoy a successful and happy life! Go within, make peace with your spirit self and don't compare yourself with anyone. Think about what brings you joy and find peace with your fellow man. Peace within brings clarity and you will begin to see yourself with new eyes. It's just like when the cataract doctor pulls out the cloudy lens with cobwebs from your eyes. Now, after all these years, I am finally seeing who I really am. And I like the man. I've learned to shift the gears better; I've moved ahead. No, not everything is clear yet, but I'm working on it, and I can honestly tell you I see every day as a unique possibility. I am filled with anticipation and enthusiasm each and every day. Friends, I wish that for each and every one of you. Shift your gears and move ahead. Go forward. Life is a precious, precious gift and you have all the tools to build a wonderful one. Keep moving and...SHINE!!!

LIFE 101

I am not a college graduate, no degree here. But in my life as a mailman I was schooled and graduated with a major in "LIFE 101." I saw it all...life, death, the good, the bad, and the ugly. Every subject there is and was and much better, yet I paid attention.

One route I had was in a very wonderful area of town, a bedroom community consisting mainly of young families. They were well educated and successful. Sometimes you would actually get to know people, other times it was a simple wave or nod. I was still young at the time and was easily impressed. One of the households included a man and a woman, both not much older than I, and they had two young children. I never really talked to the man and woman. I would see them jogging or getting into their cars. Sometimes I would see them when I brought a package to their front door. I envisioned them to be the American Dream Team. Everything I wanted to be. For months I had not seen the man and was wondering what had happened to him. A neighbor told me that he had become ill. I never really gave it much thought till the day I learned a valuable lesson...Life can change quickly.

One day I noticed a man bent over as he walked out with a small dog on a leash. As I got out of my truck, the man came up to me. I was shocked when I realized it was the athletic man who used to run and was now having great difficulty walking. He said to me, "Can you help me? I can't remember where I live." It was heartbreaking. I found someone to help get him back home. Several months later, he passed away leaving his wife and children. Friends, there are no guarantees to our days here on Earth, not in the best of neighborhoods or in the worst. Seize the day and act on it. Do not waste any time lamenting over what you don't have rather make good on what there is. Remember, today is only a passage into tomorrow and do not forget how quickly it passes. SHINE!!!

HAPPINESS IS

Do you remember the cartoon in the 70's with the caption, Happiness Is? Today I was thinking about how my ideas on what happiness is has changed over the years. When I was very young, happiness might have been a toy and when I was a teenager perhaps getting my first car and enjoying the freedom that came with it. Later, finding a career and getting married was paramount. Today, as a parent, I think happiness for me would be knowing that my children were living happy and fulfilled lives. Perhaps in coming years, my own personal happiness agendas will change. The story will be edited, some things deleted, and others added. It is an ever-changing story, isn't it? I really can't tell anyone how to find their own personal happiness. I wish I could, but it really is all up you. I used to have long-term plans for reaching certain plateaus, now I take the day for what it brings, and I do my best to enjoy moments.

Today, as the sun dipped into night, I inhaled the cool crisp air and gazed out at the landscape around me as the lovely sky retreated. Soon the moon began to rise, and I was happy to experience the changing of the guard. Little things: I try to appreciate them and rejoice. Happiness is...you fill in the blank. I hope you can and will. Shine, my friends, SHINE!!!

GOD LOVES YOU

Some of the happiest moments of my life were spending time with my children. I mentioned this story earlier about teaching my oldest how to swim. Remember when I told you that he would say to me, "I'm scared, I'm scared," and I would say, "You're safe, I won't let anything happen to you." And that is how my relationship with GOD is. I've heard some men declare that they are not afraid of anything. Well true confession: I am at times. I'm not afraid of monsters and myths, but sometimes just plain living can put scary thoughts in your head. For example, will there be enough of enough to keep my family going? Everything could go south in a minute if we experience a catastrophic event that threatens our health or financial situation. Sometimes I tell God, "I'm scared, I'm scared," and He IS THERE...AND I TRUST

HIM. His voice is calming when He tells me, "You are safe, I will not let anything happen to you that you cannot handle." Yes, sometimes, friends, I can be a little boy in a big pool that's deep called the WORLD, and I can't make it without my Father. GOD IS AWESOME! Have a great day and know GOD loves you. SHINE!!!

FIREWORKS

When I was young, July 4th meant a whole day of fun! Back then there were no electronic games to play inside, so it was all about outside. We lived in an old wooden house on a dirt road. There were big trees to climb and a large field next to our house where neighborhood friends would play games. Our mother usually fixed a special meal for us. My sister and I were given a package of sparklers that we would save for when it got dark. It was a day we all looked forward to. I know that each generation believes that they lived during the best of years, but I really think it was, especially in the early 60's, still an innocent age to be a child. And we, who lived in AMERICA, were ever, ever so fortunate. In those days, on Sundays at church, many times the names of young men who died while serving the country were called out. Being young, I knew it was sad, but I never realized what it was all about. I knew war was evil, but I never really thought about the lives that were lost, the price that was paid so I could live in a free country. Now I have been fortunate to enjoy the life of an AMERICAN living in a free society, and it is heartbreaking to see the plight of people fleeing other countries to seek the very freedom I have enjoyed. I don't know the answers. My heart grieves for their plight. There are no easy answers. Things everywhere have gotten way out of hand, even arguments over shoes. It has gotten ridiculous, like a bad dream. Thank you, GOD, for America and every freedom we have all enjoyed and sometimes taken for granted.

A few months ago, I drove back to my hometown and past where the wooden house had been. It's gone and only an empty lot remains. Sentimentality, I walked through the high weeds on the lot. I looked across the road at a neighbor's house where friends once lived. There was a children's party going on, I could hear laughter and it brought a tear to my eye. I tried to remember back when it was a windy day. If you listened closely, I swear you could hear the laughter of a little skinny boy, so very innocent. He looks quite different now. But the dreams are still in his/my heart. Tonight, I will go out on my front porch at home and look up at the fireworks. Many, many memories still live on in my heart. It's July 4th, sparkle and SHINE!!!

NOBODY IS PERFECT

My late grandmother had a drawer full of sayings. The one that rings clear in my head is, "When you have kids and animals you can't keep anything nice!" Well, she was a tough cookie. She had three sons, lived through the depression, and had a unique husband to boot. They loved each other but it had not been a cakewalk existence. In the end, my grandfather died one year before she did. She missed him every day of that remaining year! I thought about her this morning because we have three cats and one dog. One of our cats has heath issues and throws up here and there, on the rugs, in a chair, just about everywhere. It's tough to keep everything looking nice. But man, they do make life interesting. Who needs that beautiful, luxurious rug that cost me big time anyway?

The cat is looking right at me. Well? Nobody's PURRRRRRRRRRRRRRRRRRRRRRRRRFECT! Or are they? SHINE!!!

GOODNESS DWELLS IN THE HEART
AND SOUL

One of our favorite things to do on the weekend in our home is to sit and watch classic movies, most of them are from the 1940's and 50's. What really strikes me is the patriotism and faith the characters possessed in these films. In yesterday's film, they actually prayed to GOD in thanksgiving for the meal they were about to have. It was so refreshing and all I could think was how we will never see that in most of our films today. It was the early 1960's, 1963 I believe, that a famous atheist decided to create a war against prayer in the public school systems. Many decided she was crazy and didn't have a "prayer" and ignored her pursuit. She won and prayer was taken out - far out - and followers came behind her to take her place. Do I think it made an impact on our lives? YES, most certainly! It created a domino effect on things to come. I am not a rebel or a vigilante; I'd rather be a peacemaker. Still, I think there is a day and a time to say, NO, YOU CANNOT DO THAT. Everyone is concerned about keeping the planet safe and eco-friendly for the next generations. How about a planet with morals, respect, values and honor? I'd like to recycle faith, and yes, ALL faiths, there IS plenty of room. Furthermore, I'm ready to stand on this right here and now. Our country was founded on this statement AMERICA, "IN GOD WE TRUST." I value this; I believe this. If you come to our country, know that this was what we are founded on.

Yesterday's film was dramatic, but it had a happy ending. I like happy endings and I believe, at heart, most people are good and decent. Goodness dwells in the heart and soul. We need to stride to do good deeds because even the smallest act of kindness can make a difference in this world! CUT, PRINT, clear the set. Have a great day friends, SHINE!!!

LIFE IS CALLING

When I was younger, I felt that if you worked hard you would get to the perfect, most wonderful place in life where everything was just the way you wanted it to be - like my beautifully cut lawn looks after mowing. But we are a movement in time where nothing really stops to be that perfect moment forever. Weeds grow all around us. Sometimes it's not even my life that affects me but the lives of people I love, and I am helpless to change the situations. Life...happy are those who go with the flow and enjoy the good, deal with the bad and avoid the ugly. I try to find beauty in the moment with thanksgiving in my heart for all the blessings I have. I strive to care about others around me. It can't just be about me. Keep moving, find love and give love and look forward. I'm up; it's early and still dark outside. I mowed the lawn yesterday and it looks great with the help of sprinklers and the possibility of rain it will grow, and change, and so will I. Everything is filled with energy movement, so get moving! Life is calling every second of the day, SHINE EVERYONE!!!

DANCE WHILE THE MUSIC IS

STILL PLAYING

I am having a hard time sleeping tonight, so I'll write. This week is starting out to be one tough ride. I have been notified of two deaths in my extended family and informed that another family member is slowly going downhill with a debilitating disease. The caretaker, a loved one, is struggling to keep this family member afloat. Growing older for me is like being invited to party and playing a once popular children's game Musical Chairs. When the music stops, you try to grab a chair or you have to leave the game. Well friends, I've been invited to that party called the SENIOR CITIZEN CLUB. Growing up, you would hear about good news like a friend making a sports team, being select to attend a good college, or getting married and having children. Now I'm being informed on who has become ill and worse...who has died. LIFE: it's a compromise, and time can be a very tough customer.

I have a close family member that could have been the poster for Brawny Towels or a true to life lumberjack...a man with legs like tree trunks and built like a tank. When he was approaching his senior years, an illness began robbing him of his Hercules strength. Now simple tasks of everyday living have become difficult. We know it's only a matter of time before getting up from a chair and walking with a cane will become so difficult that he will not be able to do it without mechanical assistance. Knowing this reality makes me feel like I'm stuck in a dark forbidding place. It could be if I let it. Dear friends: I can't, you can't...we can't! Like I wrote, I'm at that party now, too. So, who knows when I won't find that chair when the music will stop? I have to remember that all I have to be sure of is today. Despite everything that is around me, I'm looking for some fun and I'm going to dance while the music is still playing. There is a price to pay when you love someone. Reaching out and touching someone else's life...and then they are gone. But I will keep taking the risk. There is no greater joy than to love and to have been loved. Now I've got to try to sleep. Yes, I am still invited to the party. And if you know me, I'm planning to be the LIFE of the party. Dance while the music is playing, the spotlight is on. SHINE!!!

DREAM BIG

This month I will be married for 40 years! I was 23 when I took the leap, and it was, for me, the right time and place. I was working at a relatively low paying job at the time, and to be honest I had very little money saved. I decided it was also time to buy my first place. Looking back, I realize that I've always been optimistic. Looking at my circumstances you might have said, "You are dreaming!" Nevertheless, I sold my prized possession, my beloved car, found a realtor and told her what I could put down on the deposit for a home. Today I laugh when we watch these shows where young people are looking for their first home and the gigantic budget...it must have this and that and a pool and everything that has taken so many of us a lifetime to get. I was happy to have four walls and a toilet, and I found it. I will agree that I was fortunate to get a good job and over the years was able to move up, but it never, ever was easy; a lot of overtime, a lot of driving junkers, a lot of days packing my lunch. But I believe ANYONE who is willing to work hard can live the AMERICAN dream. Nothing good ever comes easy. This was not meant to be a political post; I try to stay out of that arena. But I do believe AMERICA is exceptional, and I do believe if you are willing to work hard, you can make a good life. My first place came up for sale recently - it's still inexpensive in today's world - but worth much more than what I paid for it. I'd like to think it will make the perfect starter home for a sweet young couple and I'd tell them to just think of it as a good place to start but dream big. I'm still dreaming, but at this point a little nap or two can't hurt! Dream on friends and SHINE!!!

A BEACON IN THE DARK

Tonight, I watched an old classic "The Grapes of Wrath" and I am sure that most of you have seen the movie or read the book by Steinbeck. It is a long hard look at people being forced to leave their homes in search of finding employment to order to survive. At the present time, it makes me think of the migrants fleeing their oppressive countries and seeking opportunities here in the greatest country in the world. Friends, I am not here to argue the case. Yes, I am aware of the possibilities of criminals and Isis members being in that group. It is a clear and dangerous issue, but my heart does go out to freedom seeking families in search for a better life...and I grieve. It is a tough world to live in, if you really care. And regardless of what party you may choose, it is bazaar to think some politicians are raising millions and millions of dollars while someone will go to sleep hungry tonight...and I grieve. Time after time, age after age, there is always - and will always be - the haves and the have not...and I grieve. I don't have the answers, no one seems to...and I grieve. I'm not the kind of person who can sit in an expensive restaurant eating and watch some street person looking through the window and still enjoy my food...I grieve. So, what can we do? I honestly believe we can try to do everything in our personal life to live the right way: to respect others, to help out where we can, to obey the laws and to share anything and everything possible to keep a civil and law-biding world around us. Every act of kindness we can do will keep the possibility for a better world alive. Care about your fellow man and be a worker of the light. Darkness is out there like never before. It's midnight in the garden of good and evil.

Decide to hold a light. One small light can be a beacon in the dark. Be that light and let it SHINE!!!

EVERYDAY LIFE

Everyday life is like playing sports. Before you go out on the field the coach will tell you, "Team, I want you to give it your best!" Today I'm telling you the same thing for this and for every day hereafter. Give it your best! We all know that there ARE days when we just do not even feel like playing. There can be many reasons like when you do not like the opposing team because they don't play fair or when this or that hurts, and you'd rather not go through additional pain. It would be much easier to just take a day off. But there is a game to play, a game called LIFE, and I am a player and so are you! Suit up, get out, GAME ON. And there are NO guarantees that the other side will play fair. You make the decision. I want to play with decency, honesty, valor and respect. It will not always be easy. In my part-time job I deal with the public and believe me, you can find yourself getting tackled, brushed and called out on a foul. Friends, isn't it all how we chose to play the game? In life, I have lost many battles/games. I've struck-out many, many times, been tackled more than once, and ousted to the outfield because I was considered useless more than once. Look at me now - I am still in the game. I've survived, thrived and keep on going. Today, let's give it all we got and MORE. Here we go, TEAM, life is calling, and it is time to tackle another day and GIVE IT YOUR BEST SHOT! Much love to each and every one of you. It can be a tough game, but I have faith that you can do it! YOU ARE A SUPERSTAR. GO TEAM GO and SHINE!!!

FLIP THE SWITCH

Dear friends, one of the toughest things for me is to watch a loved one get hurt by someone's harsh and cruel words. It makes me sick to my stomach, and I have to fight not to hate back. I cannot, I will not, let myself hate, but man it's a toughie! This world is not a cake walk for most of us. Do we make mistakes? Yes. But why do people sometimes feel the need to hurt us by striking out, not by mistake but on purpose? The natural instinct is to immediately retaliate, an eye for an eye. And that leads right back to the pig pen where it came from. Done some time there before, and I don't like the smell. This is where faith steps in...hand it over to GOD. It's not an easy thing to do and not a popular thing to do these days is it? But if we are going to be our best, give our best and live our best, it's got to be done. A heart full of hate has no room for love, and without love we cease to exist. I really believe hate opens the door for poor health. We all long for justice but face it, this planet can't always deliver it. Someday in that perfect place we will know love and total peace. Here on Earth...it's a rare occasion. I hope to always be honest with each and every one of you by walking the walk, practicing what I preach. Often the road is tough, so we need to be as tough as nails. I'll be alright, I've still got my love light on...just got to flip the switch and SHINE!!!

A TRIP TO HEAVEN

This story is perhaps unusual, even slightly bazaar, but it's what someone told to me (the words may not be verbatim; after all, forty years ago is a long time). Here goes. When I was growing up, my parents were both very giving people (my mother especially, who was active in several church activities). In one of these groups she belonged to, their mission was to help the elderly, who were not able to drive, get to church. It was just about the time I began driving. Sometimes my mother would send me on errands. She was a wise woman and knew how much I wanted to drive, so why not use it for good? *Good for her,* I thought! There was this elderly woman who needed to go grocery shopping and I felt my mother used me as her "sacrificial lamb." I was told to take this lady to the grocery store. I was a little mortified. What if my school friends saw me piloting this old lady around? These kids were my classmates; one or two were pretty girls who cashiered at the grocery store we were going to. The answer was: you want driving privileges, don't you? Of course, and so I became her chauffeur. This old lady turned out to be one sharp cookie. I would wait inside of the store for what seemed like an eternity for her to shop, and then I'd help her to the car (hoping no friends would see me). After we drove up to her house, I would take in her grocery bags. Honestly, I could not wait to leave. Her house looked like a library; books were everywhere. She would insist that I take the money she handed me for a tip. I refused knowing my parents would not approve so she "made" me sit down and have a snack instead. The snack consisted of a horrible concoction she came up with and insisted it was healthy. Well, this went on for a few months. Each trip she would manage to get in a small story about her past. She had been well educated in a time most woman had not been and she went on to acquire a good position in the work force. Her first marriage had been a bad one and unfortunately, the one good thing out that came out of it was a son who had since passed away. She made two things very clear to me: how much she loved GOD and how much she loved children. After I gained her trust, she told me other stories about her life. In those days, I don't think anyone spoke about out-of-body experiences. I had never heard of any. One afternoon out of the blue, she told me she had seen Heaven. As the story unraveled, she said she had lived in an apartment complex where a young family with two small children also lived. The children's parents had asked her one day if she could babysit them while they went out on an errand. She happily agreed and to fill the time, she read them some children's Bible stories. The parents returned and later the father came over to her apartment and "blasted" her for telling his children about God. Before going, he told her to stay away from his children. She told me she cried and vowed out loud that she would never do that again and was miserable for days. She was angry at God because she wanted to know why this happened when she was doing what she thought God wanted her to do. One afternoon shortly thereafter, she was resting in a comfortable chair and suddenly the room became dark, dark as night, even though it was the afternoon and sunlight was coming through the window. Then a giant angel appeared before her and took her hand. She told me they "went" through the roof of her building and into the skies. She could see the earth below her and planets all around her. Suddenly they were in the most beautiful place she had ever been to in her life. There were trees, green grass, and the most beautiful flowers she'd ever seen. Small children were running around, playing games and laughing. Now, I can't remember the words exactly, but I believe the angel told her these innocent children had died while on earth and had never been told about God's abundant love for them. He told her that it was very, very important that she keep telling children about him. He loved each and every one of them and wanted them to know it! Before she knew it, her body was going at the speed of light and she went back into her body with a jolt. Because of this, she became a fierce advocate for teaching children about the love of God.

Like I say, back then you just didn't hear those stories. They'd come for you and lock you away. Do I believe it? I hope you can decide that in my work now. I'm not assigned children, though. I think God knows that I still want to drive...and guess where he put me!

Some believe He doesn't have a sense of humor. Think again, dear friends, think again...if He has a job cut out for you to do, He will see to it that you do it! SHINE ON as bright as the heavens!!!

CONSTRUCTION HAT ON

Growing older is like a construction site with phases. I think that I am in phase one now. In phase one, your eyesight is changing, and you require reading glasses to see small print. The good news is you cannot see all your wrinkles in the mirror. Your hearing isn't as sharp so you can't hear the comments people are whispering behind your back. You begin to slow down a little bit and begin to smell the roses (metaphorically, because the sense of smell can be affected in other phases). You can still see how wonderful life is, and how precious.

Look friends, I really don't like the aging process, but I do try to see the positive in it all. I'm still here, you're still here, so let's make good on it. After all, we can't stop the construction and the demolition, can we? My wife calls me from another room, "Steve, DID you hear what I said?" And I answer, "YES DEAR, RIGHT AWAY DEAR," even though I did not hear a thing. Got my construction hat on...check. Sometimes the right answers appear, and you hope for the best! Have a wonderful day and SHINE!!!

ABIDING IN THE LIGHT OF GOD'S LOVE

I think quite a lot about GOD. The Creator is important to me. Growing up, I was raised in a strict religious belief system, and I think now that I feared GOD very, very much. I was sure at any moment lightning bolts would hit me. Sometimes, truthfully, I merited them. Human nature is a complicated creation...isn't it? Then when I became a parent, I was suddenly in charge...well, temporarily. Thoughts came streaming into my mind. As my children grew up, there were times that tested my love in a way. But no matter where they took me, I always had a sweet memory of something they did or said as a young child and that makes me smile a big smile. I realized how very much I loved them - still do - and it was worth all the trouble. I like to think that GOD has those memories of me and you and the entire human race.

Maybe it's juvenile of me, but I keep the thought close to my heart. I need GOD'S love in my mind and in my heart. Sometimes, when I see or read about some terrible person, I try to think...they were an innocent child at one time. Dear GOD have mercy, pardon us for our shortcomings. Have a good day and try to SHINE in the light of God's love and forgiveness.

WHO IS THE ENEMY?

These days, many places of business want to make self-serve lines, check ins and check-outs to make life go faster. But I'm afraid the modern world would also like you to check in your brain and check out without your own personal thought preferences. We are often told how to think. Someone lets us know who the enemy is and who our friends are. What really, really amazes me is that so many people are willing to get in line and hand it over. I'm not, nor should you.

I was looking through some posts and found people declaring negatives about a certain person (in the spotlight of the day) and they insinuated that these thoughts were acceptable with the entire group. I can't do it, and I have come under fire for this, but I look at the heart of a person first. If they go to the beat of a different drum, so be it. As long as I see love in their heart and respect for other people's views, then they are my friend, case closed. I am not on planet Earth to sit on any judgment seat. Truth be known, I'd be alongside of the accused with my own sins. I always say, "Don't count my sins and I won't count yours." I use common sense when sizing up a person. If not, I am sure that in many cases I would have missed out meeting wonderful friends along the way. America is in a gigantic battle, a battle where sides are being drawn like never before in my lifetime. Even within my own world I really, really need to think more clearly than ever.

So, who is the enemy? All I will say is that it's the one as old as time is itself. Yes, I believe. I am working hard at keeping my heart as pure and clean as I possibly can. I guard it will all my being. Dear friends, don't hand it over and check out fast. Review your thoughts and beliefs and be accountable. Maybe it's a long line, but the wait is priceless. I wish each of you love, happiness and contentment...SHINE!!!

PICK UP YOUR CROSS AND CARRY IT

I noticed him right away. He came into the place I work, and though it was a hot day he had on an old overcoat, and though his wild hair escaped in many directions under his hat, I could see he had a distinct deformity.

When I was young and complained about this or that, my mother would say, "Pick up your cross and carry it." Even at a young age I kinda-sorta knew what she was trying to tell me. Whatever the problem is, deal with it and keep going. Of course, I didn't care for the saying, not at all. Now that I've lived over half of a century, I do understand the ramifications of what she was trying to tell me.

Most of us don't have it all, at least in my circle to be truthful. If you do, consider yourself very fortunate. There seems to be always something that keeps the word PERFECT out of my vocabulary. I've been lucky enough to have lived on both sides of the city, the poor and the affluent. Money does make a difference, but it can't promise you a rose garden, at least not a perfect one. And don't forget that roses though pretty to look at have thorn's, so be careful how you handle them. Crosses exist in this world and it is up to us to decide how we are going to do about them. Do we hide them or ditch them, or do we carry them with dignity? Honestly, I've tried to hide some of mine and ended up going back to get them. I have compassion when I see other people carry their crosses in the best way they can. Sometimes people won't let you help them, maybe because of pride or embarrassment. Been there, done that too. But if we can show mercy and compassion, I really do believe the message will come through...to love thy neighbor.

Later, I saw the man with the overcoat and hat sitting on the sidewalk. People were passing him by. I tried to talk with him, but he was not interested. I do understand. In the field of life, there are many crosses out there...some small, some big. GOD gave me strong arms and I am thankful, but dear GOD let me be stronger yet. If I see someone who needs help struggling with their cross, I want to help them if they let me. For blessed are we when we can. Pick up your cross or ease the burden of someone else who needs help picking up theirs and SHINE!!!

LIFE IS A GIVEN

LIFE is not just a fluke, a chance happening or an accident of nature. Rather, I feel it is a GIVEN. We all have the opportunity to make our mark on this map of history. Even the most obscure life can be profound. I am not famous, wealthy, or really of great important to the great masses...but my being here just might make a great difference to someone else's life.

When I was very young, maybe six, my father took a number of us children to swim in the ocean. I wasn't very good at it, but I was in the mix and did not want to be left out. We had encouraged my father to let us all get on his shoulders and jump off. A larger kid, eager to be next, accidentally kick me backwards and I stepped off a ridge into deeper water and I began to sink fast. There was no pain, but somehow, I knew that I was drowning. Suddenly, someone grabbed me and brought me to the top. It was an older neighborhood boy who saved my life. If he had not been there, all the history that I have made since that day wouldn't have existed.

Think about this: is there someone "drowning" in your world - either in or out of water - who you could help? We are all here for just that moment so why not make that moment count! Show kindness and genuinely care about your neighbor, the man on the street. It's your opportunity to do something good. You just might save a life and make history...SHINE ON FRIENDS!!!

HOME IMPROVEMENTS

Many people today are making the effort to try to change our world into a better place and I will be the first to say that there is, indeed, room for improvements. But friends, I like the term "HOME IMPROVEMENT." You need to work on your own "home" before you tear down your neighbor's walls. Our attitude, the way we treat one another mixed with love and respect, are the tools we all need, as human beings, if we are to build a better world. I don't know if I can use the word karma, but nothing good will come from hate and violence. We are losing our way in society, and one day it will crash, big time. It starts with me...and it starts with you. Have a good day and pass it forward to your family, to your friends, to your neighbors, and to people you meet on this journey of LIFE. Pass the light on and SHINE!!!

ONE SMALL STEP INTO THE FUTURE

For some time now, I've been going around and saying, "50 years ago," and I cannot believe it's been 50 years! Yes, I am getting a little tired of hearing myself say it over and over again. But it was a half century ago and I lived through it! So here it goes, July 20, 1969. I was thirteen and not really ambitious about anything. It seemed like I was caught in the middle of everything (I was still a kid) but on the fringe of adolescence. A man was going to the moon while I was about to be launched into being a full-fledged teenager. I was going to be in the eighth grade soon. And the ageless statement "If only I knew then what I know now" still applies. I don't know if it was being lazy or just unaware; then again, it really was a different age. No one I knew owned a computer and cell phones hadn't been invented yet. It's strange to think about it. I was just a naive kid. That year the movie "Midnight Cowboy" was released with an "R" rating. What was scandalous then seems rather tame in this day and age. Life was slower, I was slower too. It's my opinion that young people today know way too much, way too soon. Bear with me if you think it is just the rambling thoughts of another senior citizen. So many things were a mystery back then. I don't even know if I thought about what life would be like in 2019 or what it would be like to be in my sixties. The world keeps spinning on its axis and time is moving so fast. But would I want to be thirteen again? Honestly, no...it wouldn't suit my personality today. And I think there would be too many opportunities to get into trouble. I feel for the youth of today. Perhaps my father and his father would have thought the same thing I do now. My ambition has taken a strange turn, I embrace it. You have to be careful though, ambition can lead to burnout and sometimes a shorter life due to stress. On the other hand, maybe the crazy lazy days of summer should be equally embraced. Balance, my friends, it is all about balance. Well, let's see how I feel in another 50 years...see what ambition can do to you. Maybe I'll be living on the moon, you never know. I'd better go outside and take a look. There is always the possibility of time machines...I've heard that scientists have already built one, one small step into the future. HAPPY ANNIVERSARY, AMERICA! Until next time, SHINE ON EVERYONE!!!

A CLOSER LOOK IN THE MIRROR

Someone I know was remarking on how my face is, well, changing. Like it or not, time is making alterations and I say, so be it. We live in an age where youth is rewarded, so as we get older, we do everything possible to escape the fate of aging. Yes, it's wonderful if you can keep a youthful appearance and it benefits you to exercise and take care of your body.

On my dresser is a picture of my late father which I have a striking resemblance to. I like to feel linked to him. Time is bringing us closer, in more ways than one. I wish we could sit down together and talk. Did he feel the same things I am feeling now? Becoming older is, for me, an interesting journey. I don't know if there is an exact date on the human calendar or if you're too busy to notice but WHAM! Suddenly you find yourself in a different world, a different weight and "poof" you are part of the older generation. Overnight, I've become "one of them" an "older" gentleman. Right now, I feel like I am in the rehearsal phase, soon to take the act on the road. I remember my father, my best friend, every day of my life, and I did notice a little bit of his struggles with time. Back then, I never really gave it much thought, but now I do because I have a front row seat in the process of aging. I miss my father dearly and find comfort in the fact that he is always with me, I see him in the mirror. Here's looking at you, Dad...you SHINE!!!

BE GOOD TO YOURSELF

Being good to yourself is one of the best things you can ever do. Think about it, the second greatest commandment is to love your neighbor as YOURSELF. Loving yourself and loving your neighbor: I believe that is where you will find happiness. Loving yourself and also loving your neighbor is not always an easy thing to do, but it is the right thing to do. Welcome to Earth School 101. I have so many questions I would like to ask God about. Don't forget I was the little boy who was always asking "why" in grade school.

But to get back on my subject today. Take a moment in this day and find a way to reward yourself. Yesterday, for instance, I kept wanting to buy myself a small chocolate bar. Have you ever gotten the urge for a simple treat? Never got there, too busy, but today I am making it happen and furthermore, I'm looking forward to it. When I take care of myself, I am a better person to be better to someone else, and what can be better than that? Nothing is sadder to me than when someone cannot find even one simple pleasure in the day. Life is for the living, friends, so remember to live. Do something for yourself and find happiness in the moment. Then move on to bigger things. Besides, chocolate gives you a boost of energy and, you know, wonderful things can happen. SHINE!!!

GUARD YOUR HEARTS

It is written, "For we wrestle not against flesh and blood, but against principalities, against powers, against the rulers of the darkness of this world, against spiritual wickedness in high places." This, my friends, has always been the truth, one in which mankind fails to realize time after time. I see the battle against darkness and light at a supreme point in time. We guard our homes, our cars, our finances…which we should. But in many cases, we ignore the heart, the soul, and we give in to hatred and scorn. You cannot - I cannot - possibly grow as a human being of honor and truth if we ignore the warning signs. We are in this world, yet we cannot always be a part of this world. The minute we give into hate, we are going into the darkness. It is dark outside as I write this, but soon the light will come. I love the light and the beauty that it brings with it. Guard your hearts friends, and seek out the light, and so shall you...SHINE!!!

RIGHT WHERE YOU NEED TO BE

Of all my relationships, the one I have with GOD is the most important! Over the years is has evolved quite a lot. I was raised in a strict belief system. The grade school I attended included an academic and a religious education. Students began the day participating in a Catholic Mass. I also went to church sometimes on Saturdays and most defiantly on Sundays...unless sick or dead. It was a wonderful faith for me then, and still is for others, but now I go to the beat of a different drum...it happens. With all respect, I would say that I "freelance" now: listening, reading, and going to a non-denominational church. But for me it's not about a label or a building or a name; it's about how I worship my Creator. For me, it can't be a life that is all about me...it's ALL ABOUT US. How I treat my fellow man, how I treat animals, and how I show respect for the very EARTH we live in.

When I was young, often I would often go to church with someone whose greatest ambition was to be the first one out of the parking lot. And I, myself, have been guilty of counting the minutes to when the service is over and done. In my opinion not a way to worship, and I am not good at reciting prayers; it's like a 24-7 talking session. Usually I do all the talking. But I have stopped, listened and heard the Father speak to me. And when He does, I listen; it has helped me out of some tough situations. I have failed at quite a few things in my journey, and organized religion is one of them. Some people might say I am disorganized or confused but I feel that I am right where I need to be. I hope, dear friends, that you are right where you need to be. You might have failed at a relationship along the way but hang tight to GOD. It is my desire for you to find happiness, peace of mind, and hope in the future. I believe GOD wants that for you as well. Have a great day and SHINE!!!

MONDAY MORNINGS

I feel sorry for Monday. This day of the week has always gotten a bad rap! You know it has worn the badge of bummer since forever...back to work, back to school. Wait a minute! It should be...FORWARD to this wonderful gift called LIFE. Remember that Monday's child is "fair of face," according to the poem. So, I've got another chance to get it right, to fix, to create, and to accomplish.

Friends, whatever the day of the week it is...make it your day! I am going to savor every single minute by telling the people around me how much I appreciate them. Be grateful for being alive, for everything that is right in your life. Be thankful for the things that are like waking up, functioning and living your life to the fullest!

I like Mondays, yes, I do. Are you UP for some fun today? I am going to try to make something better happen today. Get up, get out and get going. Enjoy every day of the week, and don't forget to SHINE!!!

GETTING BACK ON TRACK

The other day, I overheard someone telling a young person to get their "act" together, and I could not help but smile...not at the situation, but at the meaning of the quote. I am 63, and truthfully, I'm not sure if I have MY act together yet. There are days when I think I am finally on the supposed right track but then I get derailed. Every day has an issue here, there and sometimes everywhere.

Friends, honestly, I wonder if anyone ever gets to that perfect place and is able to maintain it. When things are going well for me and a loved one or a good friend has a problem, then their problem inadvertently become part of my problem, if you know what I mean. My saving grace, and I wish it for you, is to realize that nightfall comes, and another day will follow. Hope, yeah, I always believe in hope for tomorrow so never give up the ship.

It's getting late now and I'm closing up shop. The moon has claimed its domain in the sky. Time to go to sleep and wait for the sun to rise. My mind is filled with the plus and the minus of the day and I am taking my wish list to bed. Looking forward to having another chance to "get my act together" on the stage of LIFE. Remember the joke when someone asked a train engineer how many times his train had gotten derailed and he said, "I'm not sure, it's hard to keep track." Funny pun, but hey you gotta use the material you got, and baby I'm using it...keep on SHINING!!!

ANNE'S SECRET ANNEX

Anne Frank wrote, "In spite of everything, I still believe that people are really good at heart." This quote rings true in my heart and soul even though I never met this wonderful young girl. She died at age 15, in February 1945, while being held captive by the Nazis in the Bergen-Belson concentration camp in Germany. Her amazing courage and outlook on life and the world despite the hardships and suffering she underwent amazes me.

In the past few days, we have heard of the sickening killings of innocent people by the hands of troubled young men. I suppose we can all choose to either hate them or pray for them. I choose to pray for them. How horrible, how sad...I honestly don't know what would make a mind decide to do this. Yet, in spite of them, I believe there are so many people out there in our world who are good and decent. Friends, even though we may not be affected personally by this tragedy, our hearts are. For these are the days when many hearts will "wax cold." Fear is lurking on every corner, cameras on most every door; it can be like black paint on a windowpane that blocks the light. Do not let your light be blocked out. Let it shine even at a time like this, even more so at a time like this. There are no promises that things in our world will become better. But, this I promise...YOU and I can make our own little secret annex a better place to live in if we look for the good in each other even in the worst of times...SHINE MY FRIENDS...SHINE!!!

SEIZE THE DAY

Have you ever gone on vacation to a great destination and wished that you would never have to check out? That's how I feel about LIFE. No matter how long I've been here I still haven't seen it all! Every day is an experience of a lifetime, so SEIZE THE DAY, friends, and claim your spot in the history of time. After all, we really are only TOURISTS. I believe the secret lies in being around or sitting next to someone interesting and remembering to check out the weather reports. Rain in the forecast? Then bring your umbrella so you don't miss out on experiencing the scenery! The SUN is out there, maybe hidden by clouds, but it could pop out anytime. If not...SHINE anyway!!!

BE A FIREFLY IN THE NIGHT

Without really realizing it, I have taken on one tough task...being positive in a negative world. I am trying my best to "shine" while the dark is holding court...center stage, up front, and out in the open. I do not think anyone can argue with me. The time we are living in has some foreboding shadows sneaking up on the sidewalk called life.

Just today there has been another senseless and devastating mass shooting. Lives taken, hearts broken...horrifying tragedies now becoming a frequent occurrence. And now, out comes the pointed finger. Who is to blame? You might not want to hear what I say, but friends, it is not flesh and blood behind the EVIL...but it is evil itself. The Bible tells us that we battle not with flesh and blood, rather with powers and principalities. There are diabolic forces battling the spirit world. No place is safe anymore: our places of worship, our schools and even a quick trip to the store can find the ancient one waiting to kill and destroy. It's not the knives or the guns but THE FORCE BEHIND THEM. I grew up in the south when guns were out in the open. You could see them in the windows of a pick-up truck, and we didn't even worry about locking our car doors. It was unthinkable to fear walking into the school yard or going to the store. The world is getting darker, nightfall has come. So, what is the answer? The only thing I can tell you is...it begins within each of us. We must be the torchbearers. Our torch is the way we treat each other regardless of the color of the skin, the faith one practices, the political party one belongs to. Light the torch by reaching out and being a blessing to our fellow man. One small act of kindness can become a profound life changing event. Remember, we are in a spiritual battle. Do not let anything dim your light; do not let the enemy win. Let your energy SHINE with love and with respect. Believe it or not, you possess much more power than you realize. Yes, the path we walk on has been surrounded by desolate shadows. But the smallest of light can lead the way. KEEP your eyes on the light, become part of the light. Like fireflies in the night...we must keep SHINING.

A KALEIDOSCOPE OF MANY COLORS

A day, in itself, is a kaleidoscope of many colors. I've had light, bright, cloudy and some dark colors because even the most wonderful life can have issues. If only I could wish things...and things would happen just like I wished. Sometimes it happens in books and movies but not always in real life. Do you ever feel that way? Life interrupts and we have to take things the way they come. Life can be like driving a fast car through the mountains. You have to hang on to the steering wheel, be alert for curves and focus on what's ahead. My saving grace has always been to keep my eyes wide open and hope for the best. There has to be hope. Hope is like a life preserver, something you can hang on to in the storm. Night is here, the day is almost over. My mind is filled with a list of things that need to be done tomorrow. It's healthy to seek tomorrow, but you need to appreciate today. So, manage the time you have left, respect your responsibilities...check, check. Finish the chores you have left. My sidekick, my little dog, is in bed waiting for me to turn out the lights. Hey before you know it tomorrow will be here. Ready, set, cameras...action! On with the show, this is it...SHINE!!!

TIME FLIES

Sometimes I can't believe how very fast the years have come and gone. There have been so many things I thought I'd be and do and live…it really has been like a daydream. I used to think I'd be a progressive type of person, move around the country, see this, do that. But in reality, I've been a steady Freddie…worked for the same company for about 35 years, continue to live in Florida and pretty much follow a routine schedule. I live in a house full of antiques. My clothes dresser is the same one I had as a child (my older brother and I shared drawers). Most of our furniture is 40 years old. I think I still have some shirts from the 1980's. What happened to progressive? At one time I accused my father of never wanting anything to change, and yet here I sit on my old chair. It's funny how you imagine your life will be and what it turns out to be verses what it is...no complaints, just thinking.

I remember observing the older people in the neighborhood where I grew up, feeling like they were so out of it with their styles, their clothing and the mundane aspects of their lives. And here I sit, a member of the club...well sort of. I can't imagine my mature neighbors back then headed to the gym at 5:30 in the morning looking out these eyes. Yes, I still think I'm all that and more until the polite nice young people say "SIR" or "Mr. Steve." I turn my head and smile even though it is evident that I have arrived. So, give me my senior citizen discount, please. Oh Well...SHINE ON!!!

DON'T THROW IN THE TOWEL

Today in church the sermon was about the Book of Job. Poor Job…calamity after calamity struck him and it seemed like everybody and their brother was telling him how to handle it or why it was happening to him. Job had been a just man and he couldn't understand why it was happening to him either. Even his own wife wanted him to throw in the towel and give up on God.

Have you ever had a "Job" moment? It's easy to bang the tambourine when the party is going your way but not so when you feel like you were never invited at all. Most of us have had some tough items in our lives, times when we are overwhelmed and start to ask, "Why, God?" The Bible tells us that it rains on the just and the unjust, some things we will never understand. The worst thing, in my opinion is to tell someone the reason "why" it happened, it is much better to say "I feel your pain" if we have been through a similar situation. Otherwise, "I am here for you if you need someone to talk with" might be more appropriate. And then there are times when you get in the slump, your buddy is driving that cool expensive car and you can't even get your clunker to turn over. Life is not always fair, not at all. I remember the saying when we were small children and we didn't like the food on our plates. Mom would give us the lecture about how all the children starving in the world would appreciate the abundance of food on our plates. Sounds lame but really true. Maybe it comes down to counting your blessings. But still I feel like life is like a menu, and disappointment is one of the dishes. I've had to swallow my share, believe me.

Dear friends, hope, faith and belief are the entrees and main courses of our meals.

By the way, Job hung in there and was blessed beyond belief. He lived to a very old age. Like I say, it's not how the book starts out...rather how it finishes. Start out with faith, embrace hope and your beliefs will be beyond your expectations. Looking forward to a new day and new opportunities...wishing you peace and love. SHINE!!!

NO MAN IS AN ISLAND

I have, in my adult lifetime, had many, many jobs. I was a humdrum person who didn't really have a mission when I was young, and like the saying goes, "You better work if you want to get ahead." One of the jobs I had was sanding down cars, preparing them to be painted. I think maybe that's what being true to your own self is all about...sanding down all the layers of life when you are finally able to take a clear, honest look at yourself. Something, I believe many people are not willing to do today. People want to blame someone else or some event for all the failings in their lives. If you really want to know, then start concentrating on yourself first and except responsibility. Our society today runs from responsibilities. Yes, there are some really crappy paint jobs out there. People afraid to show their true colors. They hide behind name calling and accusations rather than face the truth. They are accusing others of things that lie on their own doorsteps. Reassessing my own personal growth, I can see many times in my life when I fall into the same patterns, the same mistakes, and the fear or maybe just being too lazy to grow as a human being. Afraid to show the real me for fear of rejection, or perhaps fear of letting someone down. The good news is that I am capable of change and transformation when I sand down my imperfections to make my patina shine. Owning who you really are is awesome. I can see both sides of the right and the left and still be happy with my personal belief system. Recently, someone left the Shine Group on Facebook because I allowed someone to stay in the group after they questioned the validity of faith in God. I understand, but I still love and respect the person who disagrees with me. Maybe it's you, but I'm strong enough not to fear rejection, but I sincerely believe that WHO you really are is the best thing you can offer to this fragile world. We are different, unique, but we cannot deny that we are all in this world together. It's time to grow up no matter what your age is. I value each and every one of you who takes the precious time to read my posts and I value your response also. Remember the poem by John Donne...no man is an island entire of itself...SHINE!!!

HATE IS LIKE A CANCER

Hate is like a cancer...when it spreads, it becomes deadly. Mind and body work together. What you allow in your mind comes upon the flesh.

Friends, don't allow the toxic condition of this world into your being. It amazes me that so many out there are focused on what foods to eat [which is good] but at the same time allow poisons into their minds by what they watch, what they listen to, and who they allow to shape their belief systems. "As you think, so shall you be." Look for the good in everyone and above all else let goodness reflect from you and SHINE!!!

AND A ONE AND A TWO

It's raining here tonight, and rain always brings back memories of my childhood. I love the rain. I remember lying in my bed and listening to the rain come down. We lived in an old wooden house and the roof must have been as old as the house. Up in the attic my father had pots and pans that would catch the leaks. They must have worked well because I don't remember any water coming down, but I do remember feeling safe inside, nestled on the top of my bunk bed. Actually, I liked the lightning when it illuminated the room. But then I was keenly aware that my parents were in the next room. They were my safety net and I did not believe anything bad would happen because they were close by. We had so very little in our tiny old house and yet we had so very much.

When I think about the world today, I ponder why many have so very much, yet they have so very little. The 50's seemed like a simpler time. Family structure was so important. Most of my friends had a father and mother. At our house we ate meals together and talked about the day's events. We really did everything together. There was a couch and chairs in our living room, and no one went to their bedrooms until it was time to go to sleep. During the week, if we had our homework done, our parents would let us watch a show or two on the television set. On the weekends, Mom took control of the TV because on Saturday nights she loved watching the Lawrence Welk Show. My sister and I dreaded it, but we had no choice in the matter...that was that. On Sunday we ALL attended church, no options given.

The rain has stopped, the streetlight shines down on the wet pavement outside. We who dwell within our stone palaces are safe from the elements. And the pots and the pans are in the cupboards not in the attic. The times really have changed and so have I. It might be actually nice to watch re-runs of the Lawrence Show. Somewhere, someplace my parents must be smiling…"And a one, and a two"…if you watched the show you know this was Lawrence's signature lead into the "champagne music" of the day. SHINE EVERYONE!!!

THE THINGS THAT GET IN BETWEEN

It never fails...something gets in between my plans for perfection. The old saying, "There's always something" applies here. I've had two appliances give up the ghost. Well, one flat died and the other is limping to the finish line, thus putting a monkey wrench in other things that need attention. Just when you think things are going in the right direction. Nevertheless, worse things could happen. Look at our world today. The in-betweens are everywhere. My appliances are small fish in the pond of the material world. I have experienced much, much worse, financially and emotionally. I'm sure most of you have too. Everyone wants to win the lotto and live happily ever after, and why not? I'll go for that, but maybe it's all how we look at life. Do we have enough of what it takes to get through the day? Are our loved ones with us or in our lives? Do we appreciate the good things in our lives? In all my lamenting today, I looked out the window and saw the beauty of nature as a butterfly passed from flower to flower. Thank you, GOD, for letting me enjoy a simple moment of the beauty of Your Creation. It is sad that we often focus on a world filled with fighting and arguing and not on the little things that make us feel happy. Try taking a few minutes out of your busy day and reflect on the beauty that IS all around us. Be grateful for all the in-between-living in this ever moving, changing world. A world where perfection will NEVER be.

Now I have to do the dishes. And I am keeping my fingers crossed that the dishwasher (me) can hang in there for a little while longer [at least until our new one arrives]. For the moment, I'm "in between" a rock and a hard place, and all I need is a clear-running stream. Well, I've seen in it happen in old movies. Not only did they wash the dishes in a stream, but they also washed their clothes and banged them on rocks. And we think we have it tough? SHINE on like a diamond in the rough!!!

DOES MONEY RULE THE WORLD?

Usually, there is no subject I will not talk about, if asked. I have lots of opinions some that not everyone wants to hear about. But today I am going to talk about MONEY. Almost everyone thinks that money rules the world. When I was a child if a relative sent me a birthday card, more than likely there was a couple of dollars inside and it was wonderful. Then when I became a teenager and wanted a car of my own, I got a job washing dishes in a pizza restaurant at about $1.65 an hour. I was happy to have money going into my savings account. A good used car could be bought for about $1,000, a king's ransom at that time, but I managed to come up with it. Probably close to a million dishes, cups, and silverware along the way. I'll bet each one of you could tell a similar story. Money, yeah, it's a good thing to have around. There is a saying from a very popular movie, "Money is like manure...it needs to be spread around." I like that! My life has been very interesting. I've lived in the poorest part of town; I've lived in the richest part of town. There were sad stories on each side of the tracks. When you are poor and drive by mansions you think that complete happiness exists inside. "If only" you lived there, life would be beautiful. Possibly, but there are no guarantees. All the gold in the world cannot buy happiness or love. One day, I was telling a lovely lady how beautiful her expensive automobile was, and she turned to me and said, "What good is it? Everyone I loved is gone, it's just a car." You see, when I saw it parked there my first thought was *wow, what a lucky person!* I would not trade anybody in my life for that car, for that house, or for that life. There is no price I'd put on anyone I've loved. Even when my children don't seem to be following a path I'd like for them, they are still priceless! To think that GOD allowed me to be a parent to His greatest creation, friends, I sit amazed. Would more money be nice? Heck yes, but somehow I know I have what I need, I always have. I just need to pay more attention.

I think I told you that my dishwasher gave me the pink slip, but a new one is on the way. Tonight, I'm back to washing pots and pans, ahh. Remember I had a job doing that when I was younger. I knew it would come in handy someday. Sending blessings out to you today. SHINE, I know my dishes will!!!

A MESSAGE FOR ME AND YOU

GOOD MORNING EVERYONE!!! I woke up with a start this morning when a message popped into my head. It must be meant for someone - maybe me, maybe YOU. But I'll share it. This is the burning question: Does LIFE put limitations on us OR do we limit our lives? There have been times in my life when things were in the dumpster [MAYBE MY THOUGHT PROCESS] and I just accepted the results of results to be...LIFE...when all along I could have just changed the outcome by my own thoughts which could have brought different actions all along. OK, stick with me. Here is the message I received today. Believe in yourself and know that GOD wants the BEST for YOU. CLEAR your mind of everything negative and make sure YOU haven't built a wall that you can't get over. And most important do not allow anyone else to decide WHO you are! Whatever you need to do, YOU can do. Blessings out to each and every one of you. You have been uniquely formed for greatness. Believe it to be so, act on it and you will SHINE!!!

MAN'S BEST FRIEND

My dog is my best friend. Yesterday, our neighborhood was a "boom" town. Lightning was flashing everywhere, and the sweet smell of rain was in the air. I loved it. Muffy, my dog, did not. Rain pelting down and thunder rumbling frighten her as well. I understand. Our pets are one of the most wonderful gifts that GOD has given us. Being a mailman for many years, you'd think I would not love dogs, but I do. I've dealt with them all: big, small, sweet and not so sweet. My late uncle was also a mailman, and at one time he had a tough route. It had, at that time, several dogs roaming the streets free and ready to bite. One day, he met up with a tough looking dog. I think it might have been a pit bull. This dog took a liking to my uncle and became his guardian angel with a tail. He would walk with my uncle and follow him through his entire route, protecting him from every dog on the beat. My uncle would reward him with a steak on Fridays! Do I think dogs can be angels? YES! Right now, it's time to feed my little angel and take her outside. She doesn't have her wings -yet - and am I glad about that. Angels come in all shapes, forms, and sizes. SHINE!!!

KEEP THOSE PAGES TURNING

The past can be relentless, like a gossip columnist making claims on who you once were and reminding you of your limitations despite the possibilities of what you might be. My advice is: edit, discard and re-write. Go forth to publish a blockbuster hit. Who you once were is not necessarily who you will be, for YOU are indeed, the AUTHOR of your own life! Remember it's not how the book starts out, rather it's how the book ends that counts. Write on with vibrant colors and interesting chapters. Keep them all guessing...be a best-seller. Keep turning those pages and SHINE EVERYONE!!!

Acknowledgments

To my sister Bernadette, without her help my book would not have been possible.

To a dear friend Thelma Blake. She encouraged me even when I was at my lowest point and ready to give up. Thelma, you rock!

And to the wonderful, wonderful readers in my Shine Group, I value each & every one of you!

About the Author

Steve Warren is a native Floridian, husband and father of three grown sons. After retiring from the U.S .Postal Service (with 35 years of dedicated service), he continues to work part-time in his community. Steve always has a smile on his face and kind words for everyone he meets. He loves gardening and landscaping his yard to perfection and has occasionally acted in local plays.

Two Girls and a Reading Corner
P.O. Box 2404
Madison, AL 35758

www.twogirlsandareadingcorner.com

Made in the USA
Middletown, DE
01 July 2021

43481365R00146